Arab Spring and Sectarian Faultlines in West Asia

Bahrain, Yemen and Syria

Arab Spring and Sectarian Faultlines in West Asia

Bahrain, Yemen and Syria

Prasanta Kumar Pradhan

idsa
INSTITUTE FOR DEFENCE STUDIES & ANALYSES
NEW DELHI

PENTAGON PRESS

Arab Spring and Sectarian Faultlines in West Asia: Bahrain, Yemen and Syria
Prasanta Kumar Pradhan

First Published in 2017

ISBN 978-93-86618-05-4

Published by
PENTAGON PRESS
206, Peacock Lane, Shahpur Jat
New Delhi-110049
Phones: 011-64706243, 26491568
Telefax: 011-26490600
email: rajan@pentagonpress.in
website: www.pentagonpress.in

In association with
Institute for Defence Studies and Analyses
No. 1, Development Enclave,
New Delhi-110010
Phone: +91-11-26717983
Website: www.idsa.in

Printed at Aegean Offset Printers, Greater Noida, U.P.

Contents

Preface

The popular protests in the Arab world beginning in 2011 has brought about massive turbulences in the politics and security of the West Asian region. The process of transition from authoritarian political systems to a democratic system has failed to take off. Rather the process has been painful, convulsive and protracted with numerous internal conflicts, civil wars, internal displacements, rise of terrorism and extremism, military interventions, and involvement of regional and extra-regional players. The tussle between the rulers to maintain status quo and the opposition forces demanding change has taken a violent shape with both sides adopting coercive means to fulfil their objectives. New political and societal forces and actors have emerged becoming crucial players for the regional peace and stability in West Asia.

In many places, the spread and aggravation of conflicts has resulted in deep sectarian divide and unremitting violence. Sectarian politics has become more pronounced and has been manifested in places such as Iraq, Syria, Yemen and Bahrain among others. But the present manifestations of sectarian politics in the region are not entirely new and disparate incidents. Sectarianism has been used in the past by the regimes for their political and foreign policy objectives. The 1979 Islamic revolution in Iran which brought the Shias to power in Tehran was a major milestone in the regional politics. Ayatollah Khomeini's declaration to export his brand of Islam was perceived as a threat by the neighbouring Gulf monarchies. The assertion of Shiite politics following the Iranian revolution threatened the sectarian balance of power in the region. The US invasion of Iraq in 2003 which removed

Saddam Hussain and, the subsequent Shiite ascendency to power in Baghdad led to further strengthening of Shia power in the region. Iran's growing relationship with Iraq in the post-Saddam era, Syria, Lebanese Hezbollah etc. emboldens the political power of Iran in West Asia. This is both a political and ideological challenge to the authority of Saudi Arabia led Sunni bloc. Saudi Arabia perceives the growing Iranian power and the nexus in the region as a threat to its authority in the Muslim world. Thus, a sectarian political tussle existed in the region even before the outbreak of the Arab Spring. The popular protests, overthrow of regimes, violence on the streets, use of force by the regimes, spread of terrorism and extremism etc. created an environment of chaos and confusion leading to further aggravation of sectarian politics. Domestic political, economic and social factors such as long term discrimination on the basis of sectarian affiliations, economic inequality, lack of opportunities for youths, social exclusion, human rights violations etc. are some of the key factors stimulating sectarian conflict in these countries.

This book analyses the sectarian dynamics in the politics and security of three key West Asian countries - Bahrain, Yemen and Syria - since the beginning of the Arab Spring. The role of two major regional powers such as Iran and Saudi Arabia has been extremely critical in all these three countries. Both Iran and Saudi Arabia have used sectarianism as a foreign policy tool to pursue their national interests in the region. They have been found to be involved in a 'proxy war' in these countries by the way of supporting either the regime or the opposition forces. In the absence of any dialogue mechanism between them the sectarian conflicts are likely to continue and even resurface more often in future. Similarly the involvement of the two extra-regional powers, the US and Russia, especially in Syria has proved to be crucial for the security and geopolitics of the whole region. Though a number of other political, social, ideological and regional issues impact and shape the situation in West Asia, sectarian politics is one of the important issues which has become more prominent and pronounced since the beginning of the Arab Spring. Sectarian faultlines have been widening since the outbreak of the protests in the Arab world and it has affected the political, economic, security and geostrategic situation of these countries.

Each of these three countries are going through different trajectories since the beginning of the uprisings. Bahrain managed to suppress the protests though with outside support. But the internal sectarian tensions still continue to simmer with several violent crackdowns by the regime on the opposition leaders. Yemen witnessed a regime change but it still remains highly unstable. The political parties and groups involved have not been able to reach a consensus over the future course of action for the country. The advance of the Houthis to capital Sanaa and the subsequent Saudi-led military intervention has further aggravated the internal security situation. In Syria, the civil war continues as the opposition is continuing its struggle to overthrow the Bashar Al Assad regime, and the regime is using all its military and security apparatus at its disposal to protect itself. The emergence of the Islamic State of Iraq and Syria (ISIS) and other terrorist and extremist groups has clearly uncovered the sectarian nature of the conflict in Syria. But there are certain trends and drivers which are found to be common among them. The implications of a deteriorating Saudi-Iran relationship, rise of extremists and terrorists, role of militaries, external intervention, the challenge of the non-state actors, lack of political negotiations to resolve conflicts, rise of the Islamists and their nexus with the regimes are some of the important trends that have been found during the Arab Spring. A complex interplay of these local, regional and global factors have defined and strongly determined the course of local and regional political developments during the Arab Spring. The politics of sectarian alliances are likely to continue in the foreseeable future. Such alliances based on sectarian affiliations and strategic calculations will only give further impetus to the regional instability. The present level of violence and political instability points to a gloomy future for the region. All the actors and forces involved in the conflict realise that sectarian politics creates divisions and polarises the societies, and that engaging in diplomacy and political negotiations only can bring an end to these enduring conflicts. This book, thus, makes a detailed study of sectarian tensions in these three countries and analyses sectarian faultlines in the context of Arab Spring.

This book would not have been complete without the help and support of a number of friends and colleagues. I am particularly thankful to the external anonymous referees for their valuable suggestions and comments which helped me sharpen my ideas on the subject and in structuring the book. I would like to express my sincere thanks to Shri Jayant Prasad, Director General, Institute for Defence Studies and Analyses (IDSA), New Delhi, for his encouragement and support to bring out this volume. I am also thankful to Maj Gen Alok Deb, Deputy Director General IDSA for his support in the publication of the book.

I would like to thank my colleagues at the West Asia Centre, IDSA, for their support. A word of appreciation also goes to the IDSA administrative staff and the library staff. My sincere thanks to Mr. Vivek Kaushik, Associate Editor, IDSA, for his diligent efforts for the timely publication of the book. Thanks are also due to Mr. Arthur Monteiro for copy editing the manuscript, Virender Negi and Rajan Arya of the Pentagon Press for their efforts in bringing out the volume on time.

Prasanta Kumar Pradhan

1

Arab Spring and Sectarian Politics in West Asia

Sectarian politics has been a critical issue in West Asia, where political alignments along sectarian lines play a major role in the regional politics. In the recent past, a sharp sectarian division in the region's politics has become highly conspicuous. The Shia-Sunni theological differences have been converted into strong political currents, which have significantly impacted the region's political landscape. The Iranian Revolution of 1979, which brought Ayatollah Ruhollah Khomeini to power in Tehran, has been an important landmark in the region's sectarian politics. Khomeini's open declaration to spread his brand of Islam (Shiism) came both as a political and ideological challenge to the neighbouring Sunni Arab countries. The revolution of 1979 made Iran the indisputable leader of the followers of Shia Islam around the world. A large number of Shias living in the Gulf Arab sheikhdoms also celebrated the Khomeini-led revolution in Iran. Saudi Arabia, on the other hand, considers itself to be the leader of the Islamic world in general and Sunnis in particular. The presence of the cities of Mecca and Medina, the two holy places in Islam, within its territory gives the kingdom a religious and political advantage in terms of leadership in the Islamic world. The claims of both Iran and Saudi Arabia to leadership have further been propelled by the massive wealth accrued from vast reserves of oil and gas in their countries.

A political conflict on the basis of sectarian affiliations is not entirely a new phenomenon and it is as old as the faith itself. Historically, the theological differences between Shias and Sunnis have often been reflected in the political arena affecting relationships among the countries in the Muslim world. In modern times such differences have widened because of the ambitions of the regimes for power, regional conflicts, authoritarian leadership, economic interests of the states, and interference by the external players. Though sectarian differences and conflicts date back to early years of Islam, over the past decades and centuries it has unfolded in many places involving a multiplicity of actors. At present, the sectarian politics between Iran and Saudi Arabia seems to have moved beyond the differences over ideology and it has started to be seen as a clash of personalities and identities in the region.

In the current political scenario, the regimes and leaders in power have used their sectarian affiliations to draw authority and legitimacy to rule. The tribal nature of the society has helped them further to perpetuate such practice. In the absence of any democratic system of governance, sectarian affiliation of citizens has been an important source of their identity. Also, the overarching role of Islam in both public and private sphere has kept people drawn towards their own religious and sectarian roots. Daniel Byman argues that, in the region, it has often been found that the state has acted in authoritarian manner against a particular group, sect or tribe. In such cases, in the face of coercive action on the part of the state, people look up to their tribes and sects for protection against the regime's coercive behaviour. Such behaviour on the part of the state keeps the sectarian and tribal bonding alive among the people as it helps them to unite on the basis of their sectarian or other sub-national identities vis-a-vis the regime.

Throughout the world, Sunnis constitute the majority with around 87-90 percent while the Shias constitute around 10-13 percent of the total Muslim population.[1] Sunnis are in power in maximum number of countries in the Muslim world today. On the other hand, Shias are in power in countries such as Iran, Iraq and Syria in West Asia and Azerbaijan in Central Asia. The Shias constitute a minority in the Sunni majority countries. The Shias living under the Sunni dominated regimes have often complained of political, social and economic discrimination by the regimes. Often protests and demonstrations by the Shias demanding political reforms, participation in the affairs of the state, Shia religious and cultural freedom, economic emancipation etc. have elicited violent reactions from the regimes. Shia political and religious leaders have been arrested, jailed and even sent to exile. Grievances of similar nature are also reported by the Sunnis living in the Shia dominated countries such as Iran and Iraq as well. Such attitudes of the regimes reflect their narrow sectarian approach towards their own minorities. In the foreign policy front sectarian affiliation also has often been a key factor in building alliances and partnerships between the countries in the region.

The 1979 Islamic revolution in Iran was a watershed moment in the modern day sectarian politics in West Asia. Khomeini's assertion of the superiority of his brand of Islam and rejection of the Arab regimes who supported ideas of pan-Arabism came as both ideological and political challenge for the later. The Islamic revolution in Iran marked the commencement of sectarian consciousness in contemporary regional politics.[2] The Arab Gulf rulers perceived the Iranian revolution as a potential threat to their dominant Sunni ideology and a challenge to their regimes as well. Inspired by the revolution, some Shias in the Arab Gulf countries celebrated Khomeini's victory. This emerged as a serious internal challenge for the Gulf Arab regimes. In order to contain the political and ideological challenge springing from Iran, the Gulf Sheikdoms formed the Gulf Cooperation Council (GCC) in 1981. The unity of the Gulf Sheikhdoms has been reflected in their cooperation in the GCC over a number of political security and economic issues in the region.

Iran and Saudi Arabia, by dint of their ideology, political power and economic clout, exercise substantial influence on their friends and allies in the region and beyond. Clearly, both these countries have emerged as two major pillars of sectarian politics leading Shias and Sunnis respectively. But their deep involvement in the sectarian politics seems to be dividing the region and aggravating the conflicts rather than providing any credible political solution. The smaller Arab Gulf countries such as Bahrain, Oman, UAE, Kuwait and Qatar have remained friendly with Saudi Arabia. Their unity, apparent in the form of the GCC, gives Saudi Arabia a strategic advantage in the regional politics vis-a-vis Iran. Beyond the Gulf region, other countries such as Jordan, Yemen and Egypt have remained close friends of the Saudi Arabia. On the other hand, Syria, Hezbollah in Lebanon and Iraq are the major forces at present supporting the Iran-led Shia bloc in the region.

The US Invasion of Iraq and Sectarian Politics in West Asia

Since the Iranian Revolution of 1979, the single most important factor which has shaped the course of sectarian politics in the region has been the US invasion of Iraq. It led to large scale violence, political instability and created divisions in the country on sectarian and ethnic lines. Initially, the tension took place between the coalition forces and the loyalists of the Saddam Hussain regime. The Sunni insurgents targeted the coalition forces, the Shias and their religious places. Gradually, the conflict took the shape of a sectarian and ethnic one. In the process, the conflict became a struggle among the different groups for control of political and economic space in the country. The establishment of the first elected government of Nouri Al Maliki and his Shia-dominated government generated a feeling of neglect and discrimination among the Sunnis, who during the Saddam era, enjoyed patronage of the regime. Vali Nasr is of the view that the American invasion of Iraq and the subsequent execution of Saddam Hussein has liberated and empowered the majority Shia population, which has been a cause of concern for the Sunnis.[3] Marc Lynch also makes a similar observation and asserts that the Iraq war contributed directly to the rise of sectarianism in the region.[4] Many of the Baathists, Saddam loyalists and Sunnis were excluded in the Maliki regime. Terrorist organisations, militias and local organised groups emerged and clashed among each other. Among the Sunnis, Al-Qaeda emerged as a powerful terrorist organisation with increasing number of terrorist attacks. A large number of ex-Baathists also organised themselves to put up challenge to the Shia majority.

Shia religious leader Moqtada Al Sadr's Mahdi Army and the

supporters of the Supreme Council for Islamic Revolution in Iraq (SCIRI) led by Abdul Aziz Al Hakim were involved in violent clashes against the Sunnis. Talmiz Ahmad opines that in the aftermath of the American attack on Iraq, a Shia identity, separate from the broader Muslim and Arab persona has been taking shape in that country.[5] Prime Minister Maliki along with other political leaders called for dialogue and reconciliation among the groups. But, evidently, Maliki failed to bring all the warring factions to the table for a dialogue. On the other hand, Maliki continuously put the blame on the Sunni insurgents for the continuing violence. On their part the Sunnis, discriminated being out of power, accused the Shias of perpetrating violence on them.

Ever since the 1991 Gulf War, US intended to cripple Iraq and overthrow the Saddam Hussain regime. Iraq faced a lot of crippling sanctions, military intervention along with the imposition of a no-fly zone. US also adopted the policy of training and arming the local militias to overthrow the Saddam regime. Some of these groups included SCIRI, Patriotic Union of Kurdistan (PUK), Kurdistan Democratic Party (KDP), Islamic Movement of Iraqi Kurdistan, and the Iraqi National Congress led by Ahmad Chalabi.[6] Such a policy of the US came to be fructified in the aftermath of the 2003 invasion of Iraq when a lot of political voids were created leaving the sectarian militias plenty of space to manoeuvre.

The political environment of the post-Saddam Iraq became filled with sectarian under currents. After the fall of Saddam, the US-led Coalition Provisional Authority (CPA) established an Interim Governing Council (IGC) which served as a provisional government for Iraq till June 1, 2004. The IGC was a 25-member body which consisted of 13 Shias, five Sunnis, five Kurds, one Turkmen and an Assyrian. The composition of the IGC clearly reflected the dominance of the Shias in the Council. A report by the International Crisis Group in August 2003 stated that this is the first time in Iraqi history that political representation was done on the basis of country's sectarian and ethnic makeup.[7] As Ismael and Ismael say, "the first act in the establishment of an Iraqi government as a sectarian body became a framework for future developments in Iraqi politics, hence establishing the Iraqi state as a sectarian – rather than a national and unified – institution."[8]

In June 2004, the IGC and the CPA were dissolved and full powers were transferred to the new interim government led by Iyad Allawi. The first parliamentary elections in the post-Saddam Iraq were conducted in 2005. The major parties joined hands to form blocs on the basis of their sectarian and ethnic identity. For example, the Shia parties came together to form the United Iraqi Alliance, the Kurds formed the Democratic Patriotic Alliance of Kurdistan and the Sunnis formed the Iraqi Accord Front. This election clearly showed the manner in which the Iraqi politics and society were divided on the sectarian and ethnic basis. As Fouad Ajami says, though post-Saddam Iraq brought democracy, it also saw bloodshed on the streets and increasing sectarianism.[9] Politics on the basis of sectarian and ethic affiliations continued in 2010 and 2014 parliamentary elections as well, though coalitions and blocs changed in each election.

Overthrow of Saddam and the establishment of Shiite dominated government in Baghdad had its implication for the region. The Shias in the region have remained neglected and discriminated through decades. In many countries the Shias form the minority and marginalised from the top political, economic and security affairs of the state. Shias constitute majority in Iran, Iraq, Bahrain and Azerbaijan. There are a large number of Shias living in other countries such as in the Gulf sheikhdoms, Yemen, Syria, Lebanon, Jordan and other countries beyond West Asia. As Vali Nasr argues, "outside of Iran, Sunnism has long been the face of the greater Middle East, particularly in defining the Arab political culture. The Shias have been the underdogs – oppressed and marginalised by Sunni ruling regimes and majority communities."[10] The Shia revival in Iraq has given a confidence among the Shias in other countries to voice their concerns.

Iran's relationship with Iraq is the most crucial geopolitical change in the region in the aftermath of the regime change in Baghdad. The Shiite religious affiliation of both was the primary factor for their changing approaches. But Kayhan Barzegar argues that Iran's engagement with post-Saddam Iraq is not just on ideological grounds, but "in strategising the role of Shiites in Iraq's power equations and regional politics."[11] High level visits were exchanged between Iran and Iraq, and the relationship has redefined the regional politics.

Rebuilding ties with Iraq provided Iran much needed regional clout to counter balance the Sunni Arab bloc prominently led by Saudi Arabia. Further, Iran's strong relationship with Assad regime and Hezbollah provides further boost to the Shia power in the region. This alliance has now become a challenge to the Sunni bloc who fear of creation of a 'Shia Crescent' led by Iran.

On the other hand, Saudi Arabia's relations with Iraq continued to degenerate with Iraqi Shiite regime coming under the influence of Iran. Though Saudi Arabia was not very comfortable with the Saddam Hussain regime, its discomfort grew even stronger with the new Shiite-led regime in Baghdad. Saudi Arabia supported Iraq in its war against Iran from 1980-88. But Saddam's invasion of Kuwait in 1991 was perceived as aggression and unacceptable for Saudi Arabia and the relationship deteriorated following the Gulf war. Following the Iraqi invasion of Kuwait in 1990, Riyadh closed it embassy in Baghdad till the diplomatic ties were restored in 2015.

The establishment of the Shia dominated government in Iraq led to the Saudi apprehension that a traditional Sunni bastion has been lost in its neighbourhood and the Sunnis are now deprived of power by the Shias in the country. More than that, it was also felt that Iraq has slowly started falling into the Iranian sphere of influence. Other Gulf Arab neighbours were also worried that too much interference of Iran in Iraq could incite their own Shia population and that prolonged sectarian violence in Iraq could spill over to their territory.[12]

Ever since the establishment of Shiite dominated government in Baghdad, both political and religious leadership of Iraq has looked up to Teheran as a reliable friend. On the other hand, Saudi relationship with Iraq has not been stabilised even after the revival of the diplomatic ties. Saudi Arabia has, from time to time, received condemnations and criticisms from the Iraqi Shia religious leaders as well as the political class. Prominent Shia leaders Moqtada Al Sadr and Ali Sistani severely condemned Saudi Arabia after Saudi Shia leader Sheikh Nimr Al Nimr was executed in 2016. There were protest marches organised by Shia leaders in Iraq against Nimr's execution by Saudi Arabia.[13] The emergence of the Islamic State of Iraq and Syria (ISIS) in Iraq also created further rifts in the Saudi-Iraqi relationship. Iraqi Prime Minister

Nouri Al Maliki accused the Saudi leadership of supporting the ISIS.[14] He also alleged that Saudi Arabia is interfering in the internal affairs of his country and trying to infiltrate the mercenaries into Iraq to create security problems in the country.[15] Saudi Arabia, on the other hand, alleged the exclusionary policies adopted by Maliki being primarily responsible for fomenting terrorism and creating instability in the country.[16] The political gulf still remains wide between Riyadh and Baghdad despite the attempts to revive the relationship by restoring diplomatic ties.

The Shiite dominated government in Iraq condemns the Saudi military intervention in Yemen. For Iraq, the problems of Yemen should be resolved by the Yemenis themselves without any external interference. A delegation of Houthis visited Iraq in August 2016[17] and met with Prime Minister Haider Al Abadi and Foreign Minister Ibrahim Al Jaafari. Houthi delegation visiting Iraq would certainly come as a geopolitical challenge for Saudi Arabia as the visit reflects a desire on their part to further strengthen the Shiite alliance in the region. Similarly, Iraqi Shias supported the protesters in Bahrain, majority of whom were Shias. Many Iraqis came out to the streets expressing support for the Bahraini protesters and appealing the regime to stop the crackdown on the protesters. Since then, periodic protests have taken place at different places in Iraq against violent crackdowns by the regime forces on the Shias. In January 2017, Nouri Al Maliki, presently the Vice President of Iraq, accused Bahrain of 'carrying out systematic murders of opposition figures' in the kingdom after three Shias were executed after being charged with murder of three police officers.[18] A number of Bahraini Shia political leaders have also visited Iraq on a number of occasions in the past, which creates further apprehension in the minds of Bahraini and Saudi rulers of a Shiite alliance in the region.

The US invasion of Iraq and the subsequent events involving Iraq has created an environment where sectarian divisions in the country became visibly prominent. Sectarian politics has become the new norm in Iraqi politics today. The successive Iraqi regimes in the post-Saddam era have failed 'to provide a narrative of the State that effectively encompasses Sunnis and Shias.'[19] As a result, the ideological and political divide between the Shias and Sunnis has further been widened which has impacted the politics and security of the whole region.

Arab Spring and Sectarian Politics

In January 2011, Zine El Abidine Ben Ali, the former Tunisian President was removed from power following massive popular protests against him. The domino effect spread throughout the West Asian and North African region leading to further protests by the people against their rulers. Apart from Ben Ali, three other long established rulers – Hosni Mubarak of Egypt, Muammar Gaddafi of Libya and Ali Abdullah Saleh of Yemen were also overthrown by the people. Protests also took place in other countries such as Algeria, Syria, Jordan, Bahrain, Oman and Saudi Arabia. The protesters demanded political reforms, economic equality, end to corruption, social equality, employment, human rights reforms and so on. The rulers, faced with imminent threats to their regimes, responded to these protests with heavy use of force, as a result of which a number of protesters were killed, wounded, arrested and jailed. But the coercive response of the state could not deter the protesters; and the popular anger and resentment against the regimes continued to spread and aggravate. In order to pacify the protesters, the regimes made reconciliatory efforts to bring all the major parties in the conflict to the negotiating table for a dialogue. National dialogues have taken place unsuccessfully in Bahrain and Yemen. But clearly, such efforts for dialogues were too little and too late to break the deadlock and reach a solution to the conflict.

Fall of the long established autocratic regimes in Tunisia, Egypt and Libya created a vacuum in the political leadership of these countries. The political process that followed their removal could not establish a new political order or leadership which would be acceptable to all parties and groups of the society. Rather the process led to violence and political instability. The transition to a democratic system of governance miserably failed in the region. In all these countries, continuous fighting between the regime and the opposition forces has crippled the establishment of peace and order. Political instability and internal violence in the long run has created a conducive environment for the growth and spread of terrorism throughout the region. A number of new terrorist groups have emerged in the region while some existing terror groups either revived or rechristened themselves by exploiting the prevailing chaos and instability. As a result of continuing terrorism and violence, large scale humanitarian crises have unfolded particularly, in Yemen and Syria. Non-serious efforts towards political dialogue, lack of a clear vision for the nation and institution building, focus of the rulers on narrow sectarian and ethnic identities and their desire to hold on to power despite the popular protests against them are some of the reasons for the continuing turmoil in the region.

Emergence of such an unstable political and security environment further widened the sectarian faultlines in the region. With the spread of protests and aggravation of the conflicts, both Saudi Arabia and Iran concentrated to protect their interests, and at the same time, maximise their gains from an evidently uncertain and chaotic regional political and security environment. From the beginning of the protests, Iran tried to capitalise upon the instability in the Arab streets by supporting the protesters against the regimes. Iran alleges the Arab regimes to be autocratic and undemocratic, and has called the protests as the second 'Islamic awakening'[20] which is inspired by its own Islamic revolution of 1979. The Saudi-led Sunni bloc on the other hand has strongly rebuked Iran, calling the popular uprisings an internal Arab affair and has warned Iran not to interfere. With the unrest spreading from one country to another, both Iran and Saudi Arabia have continued to intervene on internal affairs of other countries in order to protect their interests. They are found to be supporting either the regime or the opposition forces in the countries facing popular uprisings. Both countries augmented their efforts to garner regional and international support in their favour. Commenting on the Arab Spring, Vali Nasr states that sectarianism is an 'old wound' in the region and the 'recent popular urge for democracy, national unity and dignity has opened it and made it feel fresh'. He says that the withdrawal of a number of Arab envoys from Syria, Saudi allegation of Iranian involvement in Yemen, Saudi redline in Bahrain, and the turn of events in Syria indicate a strong sectarian showdown in the region.[21] Daniel Byman asserts that sectarianism is a 'bitter by-product of the Arab Spring'. According to him, "the collapse of governments throughout the Middle East has opened up the political space, allowing religious chauvinists to make their play for power and influence. The spread of social media accelerates the process, enabling sectarian messages to reach a broader audience."[22] The two countries' alliance with external players in the region, mainly the US and Russia, further adds to the complexity of the situation.

Since the outbreak of the Arab Spring, several theatres of conflict have emerged in the region. The popular protests in countries such as Bahrain, Syria and Yemen gradually transformed into sectarian conflicts, leading to widespread violence, use of force by the regime and ensuing political instability. In all these three countries the involvement of Iran and Saudi Arabia has been manifested in several ways. Both countries have either been supporting the opposing factions or regimes and have been alleged to be supplying weapons and funding, besides political, diplomatic and ideological support. Their deep and deliberate involvement in the conflicts make many people to believe that a 'proxy war' between Iran and Saudi Arabia is unfolding in the region.

Key Players

Saudi Arabia

Saudi Arabia is one of the few countries of the region who has successfully dealt with the protesters and has played a major role in shaping the course of protests and subsequent developments in other countries of the region. It is argued by some scholars that the countries use sectarian cards when their regime legitimacy is questioned or when they find it difficult to control the internal turmoil. According to Madawi Al Rasheed, sectarianism was used as a tool of counter-revolution during the protests in Saudi Arabia.[23] The Arab Spring has brought major challenges for the Saudi foreign policy and Riyadh's decisions and actions have uncovered some of its the underlying intentions and priorities of Saudi Arabia. In the beginning, when protests started in Tunisia and Egypt, Saudi Arabia was in favour of maintaining status quo and, thus, chose to take the side of the dictatorial rulers. Both Ben Ali of Tunisia and Hosni Mubarak of Egypt were friendly regimes towards Saudi Arabia. Thus it was easier for Saudi Arabia to support the regimes, call for peace, stability and public order. But much to the discomfort of Saudi Arabia, the protests spread to other parts of the region such as Jordan, Libya, Syria, Bahrain, Oman and Yemen. There were fringe protests in Saudi Arabia's the Eastern Province as well which led to development of Saudi nervousness and search for an appropriate response to the emerging problems. It slowly became imminent that the protests and the regime change would leave deep impacts on the regional politics in West Asia and North Africa.

The developments in Syria and Libya, two regimes hostile to Saudi Arabia, saw Riyadh changing its previous position of maintaining status quo, and supporting the protesters against Bashar Al Assad and Muammar Gaddafi both locally and internationally. Riyadh has been particularly vociferous for the ouster of Assad (now that Gaddafi is dead), accusing Assad of 'genocide' in Syria. Saudi interests in Syria have also increased with Iran's increasing involvement in the country for protecting the Assad regime.

But the developments in Saudi Arabia's neighbouring countries such as Bahrain and Yemen exposed the Saudi double standards regarding the Arab Spring. Saudi Arabia sent its military to Bahrain under the umbrella of the GCC Peninsula Shield Force to help the Bahrain rulers maintain law and order in their territory, and for the fear of the protests inciting the Saudi Shias. In Yemen, Saudi Arabia brokered a deal between then President Ali Abdullah Saleh and the opposition. Saudi Arabia was also at the forefront of the 'GCC Initiative', which paved the way for Saleh to step down and make way for an interim government. As per the GCC Initiative, the interim government organised the National Dialogue Conference. The Houthi rebels did not agree with some of the outcomes of the conference and started their march to capture the capital Sanaa. Saudi Arabia then started the Operation Decisive Storm to push the Houthis back to the Sada province.

Thus, Saudi Arabia supported the regimes and the people as it suited its national interests. The initial support for the regimes vis-à-vis the people faded away with protests beginning and intensifying in the unfriendly countries like Libya and Syria. Saudi Arabia has been selective in its approach towards the developments in the neighbourhood. A dominant sectarian character is clearly visible in the Saudi policy. Bahrain is important for Saudi Arabia as it is a Shia-majority country ruled by a Sunni royal family. Any threat to the Khalifa family would reflect as a threat for the Saudi royal family as well. Conversely, Syria is a Sunni-majority country ruled by the minority Alawite Shia Assad family. Saudi Arabia would like to see Assad ousted from power and replaced with a Sunni regime friendly to itself. Saudi Arabia is actively supporting the Salafists in the Syrian opposition by providing them both ideological and financial support.

Saudi Arabia has also been accused of playing an important role secretly in removing Mohamed Morsi from power in Egypt. In the post-Morsi period, Saudi Arabia supports the Abdel Fattah El Sisi regime. Saudi Arabia played an important role in post-Mubarak Egypt by supporting the Salafist elements in Egyptian politics in order to bring the sectarian balance of power in its favour.

Iran

Iran has tried to capitalise upon the instability in the Arab streets by supporting the protesters against their regimes. It has called for an 'Islamic awakening' throughout the region. It has also asserted that the protests are inspired by the Iranian Islamic Revolution of 1979. A senior Iranian official has stated that what Iran wants to see is "the wave of the Islamic awakening resonated through the Islamic world as an export of the Islamic Republic of Iran."[24] But Arang Keshavarzian asserts that if echoes do resonate between 1979 and 2011, they are 'likely indirect, subtle, and multifocal' and that 'their reverberations are more attuned to the concrete local and international conditions and the constellations of social forces implicated in these monumental ongoing struggles.'[25] Negin Nabavi also is of the opinion that there are differences in the Iranian Revolution of 1979 and the Arab uprisings as both took place in different times and contexts. The Arab Spring, he points out, does not have a singular leader and it is happening in a number of countries at the same time.[26]

When protests were at a peak in Cairo's Tahrir Square, Iran openly supported the protesters against the Hosni Mubarak regime. When the

Muslim Brotherhood emerged victorious in the Egyptian elections, Iran termed it as the 'final stages of Islamic awakening' and threw its support behind the Islamists. It followed this up by attempting to rebuild ties with the new regime in Cairo – a relationship that it had severed after Egypt's signing of the peace treaty with Israel in 1979. The Iranian Vice President, Hamid Baqai, visited Cairo in August 2012 and met President Morsi to indicate his country's desire to build up ties with Egypt and start a fresh chapter in bilateral relations. But it is not clear how far the new Egyptian government will go in forging a robust relationship, given the tremendous pressure against such a move from countries such as Saudi Arabia and the United States.

Similarly, Iran supported the protesters in Libya against the Gaddafi regime, while at the same time condemning the American and Western design of strengthening their foothold in that country. The protests in Bahrain brought another opportunity for Iran to strengthen its attack against the incumbent Arab regimes. The Gulf countries and Saudi Arabia in particular have alleged that Iran attempted to exploit its links with some Shia groups in Bahrain, though without producing evidence to that effect.[27] Iran has also tried to internationalise the Bahrain issue by raising it at the Organisation of Islamic Cooperation (OIC) and the United Nations. And when Saudi and UAE forces entered Bahrain to quell the protests there, Iran called it an 'intervention'.

However, Iran's tone and tenor changed when protests erupted in Syria against the regime of its ally Assad. Assad, an Alawite Shia, has enjoyed Iran's support. Instead of condemning the regime and supporting the protesters, Iran appealed for a national dialogue between the government and the protesters. While Iran has been protecting Assad, the Gulf Arab leaders, who successfully protected the ruler of Bahrain from the protests, have called for Assad's immediate removal, ending the violence and restoring peace in the country. For the Arabs, the fall of the Assad regime will weaken Iranian influence in the Levant and West Asia, while for Iran, Syria under Assad is an important ally to check the Israeli threat and sustain its own influence in the region. The Russian and Chinese vetoes in the UN Security Council over the resolution on Syria have come to Iran's aid for the time being.

Turkey

Turkey views the Arab Spring as an opportunity to spread its influence in the region, where it nurtures an ambition to play a leadership role. Turkey condemned the Mubarak regime right from the beginning and supported the Egyptian protesters. Turkey aimed to strengthen ties with the Muslim Brotherhood regime. Recep Erdogan was given a warm welcome during his visit to Cairo as part of his Arab Spring tour. Turkey intended to capitalise upon the Muslim Brotherhood's views on Israel and draw Egypt closer towards it especially in the context of its own strained relationship with Israel over the Gaza Flotilla issue.

But developments in Libya and Syria posed severe challenges to Turkish foreign policy. The challenge was how to deal with these highly polarised states, where Turkish economic interests are very high. Thus the leadership confronted an 'ethics versus self-interest' dilemma at the beginning of the Arab Spring.[28] Turkey enjoyed a warm relationship with Syria. Total bilateral trade stood at over US$ 2.5 billion and a free trade zone agreement had also been concluded. But the protests in Syria triggered Turkish concerns about a mass exodus of refugees. As a result, it initially reacted with caution and advised Assad to initiate reforms and liberalise the draconian laws. But by the time Assad offered a national dialogue to his people, it was clearly too late for the latter to accept. With the situation slowly slipping out of control, Turkey changed its approach and began to adopt an anti-Assad stand. It now wants Assad to go, thus paving the way for peace and stability. This relatively quick change of stand reflects the Turkish 'preference for instrumentalism and pragmatism over a principled foreign policy'.[29] By changing its stand, Turkey chose to side with the US and its European allies while at the same time impressing the Arabs. Ankara is now an important player in the Syrian crisis as has been affected by challenges emanating from Syria. The security challenge of the ISIS is one of the major threats facing Turkey currently. ISIS has also launched attacks inside Turkey in the recent past, killing hundreds of people. As a part of the US-led coalition, Turkey has also taken part in the airstrikes against ISIS targets in Syria. Turkey is also reportedly supporting the Syrian opposition against the Assad regime. Further, Turkey is hosting more than 2.7 million Syrian refugees, which itself is a big challenge.[30]

But Turkey faces the most important security challenge from the Kurds, who have become more active after the establishment of the 'caliphate' by the ISIS. The Kurds in Turkey continue to face the wrath of the Turkish military as the government is not ready to grant them any sort of independence or autonomy in its territory. The Kurds have started an armed struggle in the southern border area of the country led by the *Partiya Karkeren Kurdistan* (PKK – Kurdistan Workers' Party). The Turkish government has often launched military strikes against the Kurdish hideouts in Turkey and neighbouring Iraq.[31] Unlike Iraq, Turkey does not want to countenance any possibility of collaborating with the Kurds against the ISIS. After months of indecision, the Turkish government finally decided to take part in the US-led coalition in military operation against the ISIS in July 2015.[32] It allowed the coalition forces to use its Incirlik airbase, which is close to its border with Syria, for operations against the ISIS. Turkey wants the US to target the Kurds simultaneously while launching attacks against the ISIS, but the US supports the Syrian Kurds in their fight against the ISIS,[33] an approach it has adopted in Iraq where the Iraqi regime, the Kurds and other tribal forces loyal to the regime have been brought together to fight the ISIS.

The Kurds in Syria have achieved significant gains, taking advantage of the ongoing civil war. The People's Protection Units, locally known as the *Yekîneyên Parastina Gelý* (YPG), are the military branch of the Syrian Kurdistan operating under their government led by the *Partiya Yekîtiya Demokrat* (Democratic Union Party, PYD). They call their uprising as the Rojava (literally meaning, western Kurdistan) Revolution.[34] The YPG has captured and held on to the Kurdish-dominated areas in northern Syria after the regime's forces withdrew in 2012. Severe clashes have been witnessed between the YPG and the ISIS in their struggle to occupy territory in northern Syria. The Syrian Kurds have declared autonomy and intend to remain with a democratic Syria in future.[35] The Turkish government apprehends that declaration of autonomy by the Syrian Kurds may stoke similar demands from the Turkish Kurds. This perception affects the US-Turkey relationship.[36] Thus the continuing chaos in Syria has been beneficial for the Syrian Kurds. The longer the conflict continues, they get more time to entrench and consolidate their gains.[37]

Qatar

Qatar has emerged as a new force keen to play a role in the issues affecting the region. Qatar did not face a single day of protest even when the Arab streets elsewhere were burning with the popular protests and severe government crackdown. Qatar's political stability and economic wealth are two important motivating factors for it to play a proactive role in the region.[38] To ensure calm in his country, the Emir of Qatar announced a number of social and economic benefits for the people, including a substantial hike in the salary of government servants. Qatar thereafter looked to making interventions in the affairs of the region. Qatar has mediated in a number of regional conflicts, including in Sudan, Lebanon and Yemen.[39] By mediating in conflicts Qatar wants 'to contain those conflicts and prevent their spreading closer to home' and also to expand its influence throughout the region vis-à-vis its powerful neighbour, Saudi Arabia.[40] Qatar's first intervention came when the situation in Libya deteriorated. It supported the no-fly zone in Libya, overthrow of the Gaddafi regime and establishment of an authority led by the Libyan opposition. Qatar became the first Arab country to recognise the Libyan rebels as the sole representative of the Libyan people.[41] Qatar also provided them with weapons, training, funds and other logistical support. Qatar also joined the international military operation in Libya and became the first Arab country to send fighter aircraft to Libya to enforce the no-fly zone.[42] Qatar also sent hundreds of troops to fight against Gaddafi.[43] In April 2011, Qatar hosted a meeting of the international contact group on Libya. Qatar continues to have significant influence in Libya in political and security matters.

Qatar has also been at the forefront of the international anti-Assad coalition in Syria and has been vocal in forums such as the UN and Arab League to put more pressure on the regime. Qatar has also sent arms for the Syrian rebels.[44] Qatar has developed a strong connection with the Muslim Brotherhood in Syria and has been a main force behind its financial and military powers. Nevertheless, given the complex state of affairs in Syria because of the conflicting interests of the external powers, regional powers, and lack of unity among the opposition forces, it may not be easy for Qatar to manoeuvre in Syria.

Qatar supported the Muslim Brotherhood-led government in Egypt and strengthened its ties and influence with the new government. Qatari Prime Minister Hamad Bin Jassim visited Cairo in January 2013 and announced provision of huge amount of loans to Egypt to deal with the financial crisis the country was going through. During the visit, he stated: "When we reach out to a leading regional state like Egypt, we do so with an eye on helping Egypt out. We don't pay much attention to the political incitement that some are trying to ignite."[45] But Qatar suffered a huge blow in Egypt when Morsi was forced out of power by the military led by El Sisi. Nevertheless, Qatar remains a major backer of the Muslim Brotherhood in Egypt.

Changing Geopolitical Context and the Saudi-Iran Sectarian Confrontation

The P5+1 Nuclear Deal with Iran

For more than a decade the Iranian nuclear issue remained at the centre of the strategic environment in the Gulf region. Acquiring nuclear weapons would have given Iran a strategic advantage over its arch rival Saudi Arabia and other GCC countries. The GCC states also feared that nuclear weapons would give a huge military advantage to Iran and were in favour of the imposition of sanctions on that country by the US and the West. Nevertheless, the P5+1 states (China, France, Russia, UK, US and Germany) went ahead with signing a nuclear deal with Iran in July 2015. The signing of the Joint Comprehensive Plan of Action (JCPOA) between P5+1 and Iran would gradually waive off the Western sanctions on Iran, which would give Iran more economic and political freedom. The JCPOA intends to make the Iranian nuclear programme a peaceful one. Iran has also reaffirmed that it will not develop or acquire nuclear weapons. It has agreed to keep its uranium enrichment to a maximum level of 3.67 percent from the earlier 20 percent for the next 15 years. It has also agreed not to engage in research and development activities which would contribute to nuclear explosive devices.[46]

Saudi Arabia is worried that the removal of international sanctions from Iran will facilitate higher growth of the Iranian economy.[47] After the sanctions are removed Iran would get greater access to international energy markets, thus challenging the existing Saudi dominance as the top global energy exporter. Removal of sanctions will also attract a lot of foreign direct investment to Iran, which will provide the much-needed boost to the Iranian economy. This Saudi concern has alarmingly come true for the kingdom, as a number of European governments and companies have come forward to talk to Iran within months of the signing of the nuclear deal. Unhindered growth of its economy would give Iran a geopolitical advantage over Saudi Arabia. Therefore, Saudi Arabia has called for stricter sanctions from the US and West rather than a nuclear deal with Iran. An economically empowered Iran with improved trade links with the West throws up an economic and strategic challenge to the authority of Saudi Arabia in the whole region. On the other hand, the GCC countries have been feeling the pinch with the drastic fall in of global oil prices. With the current oil price oscillating between US$ 50-55 per barrel, and market analysts predicting not so rapid increase in oil prices in the near future, the GCC economies are certainly going to be negatively affected. Even an economy as big as that of Saudi Arabia has started rationing its national budget.

With the signing of the JCPOA, the tumultuous US-Iran relationship has also undergone a strategic transformation. The US-Iran rivalry was a critical factor in the political and strategic environment in the Gulf region. This kept the US closely on the side of Saudi Arabia and the other GCC states. The US remains the primary security provider in the Gulf region. It maintains military bases in all the GCC countries. But now, the US, while courting Iran with the nuclear deal, has been perceived to be 'abandoning traditional Arab allies, without establishing a credible security architecture in the region to contain and roll back Iran.'[48] Saudi Arabia fears that the growing US-Iran proximity may disturb the existing balance of power in favour of Iran. Riyadh, therefore, has been found adopting a more aggressive diplomatic approach trying to convince the US of its unremitting commitment for the Gulf security. The US, on its part, has assured its Gulf allies of its commitment towards Gulf security but the GCC countries remain unconvinced.

Another major Saudi concern is that the JCPOA does not completely abandon the Iranian nuclear programme: it only delays and slows down the process by 15 years. The Saudis also consider the deal to be unfavourable to the traditional Arab allies of the US in the region.[49] There is also a growing concern that this may lead to a nuclear arms race in the region. Saudi Arabia has in the past threatened to go nuclear if Iran were not stopped from acquiring nuclear weapons. In May 2015, Prince Turki bin Faisal, Saudi Arabia's former intelligence chief, stated: "Whatever the Iranians have, we will have, too",[50] clearly stating his country's position on the Iranian nuclear issue. A month later, in June 2015, Prince Mohammed bin Nawwaf bin Abdulaziz Al Saud, the Saudi Ambassador to London, stated that "all options are on the table"[51] if Iran became able to make nuclear weapons. As Saudi Arabia views Iran as its most powerful regional rival, Iran acquiring nuclear weapons may also trigger a nuclear arms race in the region.

The immediate eagerness of a number of European countries to do business with Iran in the aftermath of the JCPOA deal has also made Riyadh anxious. Earlier, Obama's 'pivot to Asia' policy generated apprehensions in the Gulf regarding the seriousness of the US to engage with the region, as the US was seen to be shifting its strategic priorities from West Asia to the South China Sea. The presence of the US in the region is one of the critical issues of conflict between the GCC and Iran. While the GCC wanted continued US presence in the region with its military in the Gulf, Iran proposed a regional security architecture minus any external powers. In the present context, while Iran is trying to consolidate the gains it has accrued from the signing of JCPOA, Saudi Arabia and other GCC states remain worried about a rejuvenated Iran emerging out of a harsh sanctions regime.

Politics of Military Coalitions

Saudi-led military coalition: Both Saudi Arabia and Iran have been attempting to gain more political, diplomatic and military support in their own favour. In December 2015, Saudi Arabia announced a coalition of 34 Islamic countries – all of them belonging to the OIC – to fight terrorism in the region. This initiative is intended to have a coordinated action by the countries concerned against terrorism. Saudi Deputy Crown Prince Muhammad Bin Salman stated on the occasion that, "The formation of the Islamic military alliance emanates from the Islamic world's keenness to fight terrorism and be a partner of the world in the fight against this scourge."[52] He also stated that the coalition would not focus on any particular groups but would also keep in view terrorist groups across the globe; and that the alliance would operate under the UN and OIC counterterrorism provisions.[53] This is a major Saudi initiative to build an alliance against the IS by inviting Islamic countries from West Asia, Africa and South Asia. This initiative reflects a growing concern in Riyadh about the developments taking place in the region and to play a proactive role to defend themselves.[54] But the formation of the coalition with deliberate omission of Iran limits its capabilities to achieve its intended objective of fighting terror.[55] Further, the members of the coalition are Arab/Islamic countries that are mostly friendly in their approach towards Riyadh.

Operation North Thunder: In February 2016 Saudi Arabia started Operation North Thunder at the King Khaled Military City (KKMC) at Hafr Al Batin, Saudi Arabia, which included militaries from 20 Arab and Islamic countries. The participating countries included Saudi Arabia, UAE, Jordan, Bahrain, Senegal, Sudan, Kuwait, Maldives, Morocco, Pakistan, Chad, Tunisia, Comoro Islands, Djibouti, Oman, Qatar, Malaysia, Egypt, Mauritania, and Mauritius.[56] King Salman stated that Operation North Thunder manoeuvres "raised the level of combat readiness and helped assess the ability to manage military operations to achieve the unity of ranks and ward off dangers facing Arab and Islamic nations."[57] The Saudi Chief of General Staff, General Abdulrahman bin Saleh Al Bunyan, who led the exercise, described Operation North Thunder as one of the 'biggest military exercises' (i) in terms of the number of troops participating in the operation and (ii) the extensiveness of the area of military operation.[58] It was clear to observers that Saudi Arabia's veiled political intention in taking up this initiative was to flaunt the political and military support it enjoys in the region vis-à-vis Iran.

Arab League and the Proposal of a Joint Arab Military Force: With the aggravation of conflicts in the region in the aftermath of the popular protests, the Arab League has been activated. The organisation has hitherto been perceived as an ineffective body without any real powers.

In order to show its effectiveness, legitimacy and acceptability among the people, it has been trying to rejuvenate itself in the wake of significant changes taking place throughout the region. As the popular protests slowly began to spread and intensify in the region, one of the critical moves of the body came in 2011 when it condemned the responses of Gaddafi and supported the rebels fighting against his regime. The Arab League supported the United Nations Security Council (UNSC) in imposing a no-fly zone over Libya. It also sided with the opposition forces against the Assad regime in Syria. The Arab League suspended the membership of Syria and has supported Assad's removal from power. In November 2011, the League officially recognised the National Coalition of Opposition Forces of Syria. It imposed sanctions on Syria, which include a ban on banking and trade as well as travel ban on officials.[59] But no such action has been taken by the Arab League towards the conflict and instability in other Arab countries such as Yemen, Bahrain and Egypt. This shows the selective interference by the organisation and establishes the fact that the League still operates under the influence of the wealthy and powerful Arab nations.

The emergence and growing influence of the ISIS has alarmed the Arab League. It has condemned the ISIS's establishment of a 'caliphate' in Iraq and Syria and has called upon its members to tackle the outfit 'militarily and politically'.[60] It has also strongly condemned the ISIS's destruction of cultural heritage, calling it an 'odious crime'.[61] However, member countries of the League have failed in forging any military coalition against the ISIS. Besides Iraq and Syria, the worsening situation in Libya due to continually increasing ISIS influence there is also another major concern for the Arab League. Taking the opportunity of the absence of a strong central authority in Libya, the ISIS has captured a large swath of territory in the north of the county. The internationally recognised government of Libya has not been able to check its activities and has sought the intervention of the Arab League to defeat it, without any noteworthy intervention by the latter.[62] Amidst the growing tensions in Syria, Iraq, Libya, Yemen and elsewhere, there has been a call by the countries of the region to form a joint Arab military force to face the security challenges, but Iraq is not in favour of the idea and has expressed the belief that such a force may create further insecurity in the region.[63] This issue was discussed in detail in the 26th Arab League Summit held in Sharm El Sheikh, Egypt, in March 2015 and the majority of the member states were in favour. In May 2015, Egyptian Foreign Minister Sameh Shokri stated that "a vision to establish a joint Arab force" would be 'ready within the next four months',[64] but the idea is yet to fructify.

If indeed the idea takes off effectively, it will have repercussions for the regional politics by keeping the Arab states united in the face of a common security challenge emerging in the region. Also, their relationship with Iran will be affected. But divisions remain within the Arab ranks. For instance, Oman has differences over the regional politics with its neighbours such as Saudi Arabia. Qatar also has differences of opinion on several issues with Saudi Arabia and the UAE. Egypt has differences with Qatar over the Muslim Brotherhood. Assad of Syria is not liked by many of his Arab neighbours. Similarly, the current government in Baghdad is seen by its Arab neighbours to be under the heavy influence of Iran, and thus not to be trusted completely.

Iran on the other hand has made its alliance with Iraq, Syria and Hezbollah even stronger. In September 2015, to establish a coordinated framework, Iraq, Syria, Iran and Russia formed an intelligence committee in Baghdad to coordinate the actions against the ISIS. The committee would be involved in sharing and analysing information as well as monitoring the movements of terrorists.[65] The involvement of Russia – the only extra-regional power in the group – comes because of the growing Russian concern for its nationals joining the ISIS. Russia has reportedly stated that around 2,400 of its nationals have joined the terrorist group.[66] Though the ISIS is a common enemy for all, the formation of this coalition for intelligence sharing excludes other countries of the region. This reflects the existence of deep political and sectarian division among the principal regional powers Iran and Saudi Arabia.

Saudi Arabia Severs Ties with Iran

The execution of Sheikh Nimr Al Nimr, a Shia cleric, by the Saudi authorities along with 46 others in January 2016 has led to a political and diplomatic crisis in the whole region. When Iran condemned the development,[67] Saudi Arabia described it as interference in a Saudi internal issue. After a group of protesters forcibly entered the Saudi embassy in Tehran and its consulate in Mashhad, Saudi Arabia severed all diplomatic ties with Tehran.[68] Saudi Arabia received support from its neighbours such as UAE, Bahrain and Kuwait, who also followed it in recalling their envoys from Tehran. Saudi Arabia also used its political clout in regional organisations such as the GCC, Arab League and OIC, who also condemned the attack on the Saudi embassy in Iran. Yemen and Sudan also condemned the incident. Iraq has stood by Iran in the matter and this has further deepened the Saudi-Iran rivalry.

Involvement of Extra-regional Players

The involvement of external powers in the region has added further fuel to the Saudi-Iran rivalry. At present, the US and Russia are the major extra-regional players whose involvement has been impacting the peace and stability in the region. Their divergent geopolitical and strategic interests have further divided the regional politics. The US has supported Saudi Arabia and its friendly GCC countries. There is a convergence of views of the US and Saudi Arabia in Libya, Egypt, Yemen and Syria. Thought the US did not favour the Saudi military intervention in Bahrain, the issue has been amicably sorted out between the two. Besides, the US has remained the most powerful external player throughout the region. The US intends to maintain and protect its interests in the region as the region is passing through a period of turmoil. The signing of the JCPOA has brought the US and Iran closer to a working relationship but Saudi Arabia and the GCC states still remain America's trusted allies in the region. Russia's involvement in the Syrian crisis has also changed the geopolitical situation in the region. In Syria, the opposition is demanding removal of the Assad regime. The opposition has started a political as well as armed struggle to remove Assad from power. The opposition is backed by the US and its Arab Gulf allies, who also want a regime change in Syria. But they have met with a strong challenge in Syria as Russia has come out openly supporting the Assad regime. Russia has sent its military to Syria in support of Assad regime. Russia, certainly, has a number of strategic interests in Syria. It is the only country in the region where Russia has a military base. Russia's open declaration of support to Assad challenges the US and its Gulf Arab allies in Syria which further escalates the conflict in Syria.

Conclusion

During the last six years, a lot of changes have been witnessed in the region. Relations between countries have changed, new forces have emerged, regional security has been challenged, terrorism and extremism has taken deep roots and the regional geopolitical situation has been undergoing a change. But the purpose for which the people came out to the streets to protest has not been realised. Arab Spring has created an environment which has become conducive for sectarian tensions to flare throughout the region. It has created new sectarian hotspots which have converted into frontlines of Saudi-Iranian proxy wars. Sectarian conflicts in countries like Yemen and Syria have worsened and is likely persist in the foreseeable future. Their societies and politics have been polarised on sectarian lines, thereby making it difficult for them to reach a negotiated political solution. In other places such as Bahrain, Iraq and Egypt, though the situation is not so alarming, the simmering societal tension on sectarian lines keeps open potential for conflict.

The faultlines of regional conflicts in West Asia have clearly been drawn. The actors and stakeholders have now organised themselves benefits from the chaotic political and security environment. The situation gets worsened day by day, with little sign of the tensions ebbing. This again provides an emotional and political context for further spread of sectarian conflicts in the region. The regional and extra-regional players are more driven by their national interests than for providing solutions to the conflicts. Their involvement has further complicated the situation. There is a need to contain and end the violence before the sectarian conflicts aggravate and spread further into the region and beyond.

END NOTES

1. "Mapping the Global Muslim Population", Pew Research Center, October 7, 2009, at http://www.pewforum.org/2009/10/07/mapping-the-global-muslim-population/.
2. Talmiz Ahmad, *Turmoil in West Asia: The Sectarian Divide Shapes Regional Competitions*, IDSA, New Delhi, 2016, p. 7.
3. Vali Nasr, "When the Shiites rise", *Foreign Affairs*, 85 (4), July/August 2006, pp. 58-74.
4. Mark Lynch, *The Arab Uprising: The Unfinished Revolutions of the New Middle East*, Public Affairs, New York, 2012.
5. Talmiz Ahmad, *The Islamist Challenge in West Asia: Doctrinal and Political Competitions after the Arab Spring*, Pentagon Press and IDSA, New Delhi, 2013, p. 98.
6. Tareq Y. Ismael and Jacqueline S. Ismael, *Government and Politics of the Contemporary Middle East: Continuity and Change*, Routledge, New York, 2011, p. 216.
7. "Governing Iraq", International Crisis Group, Report No. 17, August 25, 2003, at https://d2071andvip0wj.cloudfront.net/17-governing-iraq.pdf.
8. Ismael and Ismael, n. 6, pp. 216-217.
9. Fouad Ajami, "The Arab Spring at one: A year of living dangerously", *Foreign Affairs*, March/April 2012, pp. 56-65.
10. Vali Nasr, "Regional implications of Shi'a revival in Iraq", *The Washington Quarterly*, 27 (3), 2004, p. 9.
11. Kayhan Barzegar, "Iran, New Iraq and the Persian Gulf Political-Security Architecture", *The Iranian Journal of International Affairs*, 20 (1), Winter 2007-08, pp. 93-110.
12. Prasanta Kumar Pradhan, "Power vacuum and impending regional race in Iraq", IDSA Comment, September 09, 2010, at http://www.idsa.in/idsacomments/Powervacuumandim pendingregionalraceinIraq_pkpradhan_090910.
13. "Iraq's Sistani condemns Nimr execution, Sadr organizes protests", *Reuters*, January 3, 2016, at http://www.reuters.com/article/us-saudi-security-iraq-idUSKBN0UH06L20160103.
14. "Maliki accuses Saudi Arabia of backing rebels", *Al Arabiya*, June 17, 2014, at http://english.alarabiya.net/en/News/middle-east/2014/06/17/Maliki-blames-Riyadh-for-rebellion-against-him.html.
15. "Iraqi PM Nouri Maliki accuses Saudis of 'interference'", *BBC*, April 25, 2014, at http://www.bbc.com/news/world-middle-east-27162878.
16. "Saudi Arabia rejects Iraqi accusations of Isis support", *The Guardian*, June 19, 2014, at https://www.theguardian.com/world/2014/jun/19/saudi-arabia-rejects-iraqi-accusations-isis-support.
17. "Yemen's Houthi rebels seek new friends in Baghdad", *Al Araby*, August 31, 2016 at https://www.alaraby.co.uk/english/news/2016/8/31/yemens-houthi-rebels-seek-new-friends-in-baghdad.
18. "Maliki slams Bahrain after execution of 3 Shias over police murder", *Iraqi News*, January 17, 2017, at http://www.iraqinews.com/arab-world-news/maliki-

slams-bahrain-execution-3-shias-police-murder/.

19. Fanar Haddad, *Sectarianism in Iraq: Antagonistic Visions of Unity*, Hurst & Company, London, 2011, p. 38.
20. See Payam Mohseni, "The Islamic awakening: Iran's grand narrative of the Arab uprisings", *Middle East Brief*, No. 71, April 2013, Crown Center for Middle East Studies, Brandeis University, Massachusetts, at http://www.brandeis.edu/crown/publications/meb/MEB71.pdf.
21. Vali R. Nasr, "If the Arab Spring turns ugly", *The New York Times*, August 27, 2011, at http://www.nytimes.com/2011/08/28/opinion/sunday/the-dangers-lurking-in-the-arab-spring.html?_r=0.
22. Daniel Byman, "Sectarianism afflicts the New Middle East", *Survival: Global Politics and Strategy*, 56 (1), 2014, pp. 79-100.
23. Madawi Al Rasheed, "Sectarianism as counter-revolution: Saudi responses to the Arab Spring", *Studies in Ethnicity and Nationalism*, 11 (3), 2011, pp. 513-526.
24. Cited by Naysan Rafati in "Iran and the Arab Spring", London School of Economics and Political Science, at http://www2.lse.ac.uk/IDEAS/publications/reports/pdf/SR011/FINAL_ LSE_IDEAS__IranAndArabSpring_Rafati.pdf.
25. Arang Keshavarzian, "Beyond 1979 and 2011: When comparisons distract", *International Journal of Middle East Studies*, 44 (1), 2012, p. 160.
26. Negin Nabavi, "The 'Arab Spring' as seen through the prism of the 1979 Iranian Revolution", *International Journal of Middle East Studies*, 44 (1), February 2012, pp. 153-155.
27. See Atul Aneja, "Iran and the Arab Spring", *The Hindu*, July 6, 2011.
28. Ziya Onis, "Turkey and the Arab Spring: between ethics and self-interest", *Insight Turkey*, 14 (3), 2012, p. 46.
29. Sebnem Gumuscu, "Turkey's reactions to the Arab Spring", *Yale Journal of International Affairs*, May 16, 2012, at http://yalejournal.org/2012/05/turkeys-reactions-to-the-arab-spring/.
30. UN High Commission for Refugees, at http://data.unhcr.org/syrianrefugees/country.php?id=224.
31. "Why Turkey is fighting the Kurds who are fighting ISIS", *The New York Times*, August 12, 2015, at http://www.nytimes.com/interactive/2015/08/12/world/middleeast/turkey-kurds-isis.html?_r=0.
32. "War with ISIS in Iraq and Syria: Turkey joins West as a reluctant ally – but what took it so long?", *The Independent*, July 25, 2015, at http://www.independent.co.uk/news-19-6/war-with-isis-in-iraq-and-syria-turkey-joins-west-as-a-reluctant-ally-but-what-took-it-so-long-10414801.html.
33. "Turkey uneasy as U.S. support of Syrian Kurds grows", *The New York Times*, June 29, 2015, at http://www.nytimes.com/2015/06/30/world/middleeast/turkey-uneasy-as-us-support-of-syrian-kurds-grows.html.
34. Evangelos Aretaios, "The Rojava Revolution", *Open Democracy*, March 15, 2015, at https://www.opendemocracy.net/arab-awakening/evangelos-aretaios/rojava-revolution.
35. Robert S. Ford and Ali El Yassir, "The Kurdish PYD & the challenge of rebuilding a Syrian state", Middle East Institute, August 25, 2015, at http://www.mei.edu/content/at/kurdish-pyd-and-challenge-rebuilding-syrian-state.

36. Ibrahim Al Marashi, "The contest between two quasi-states: ISIL and Rojava", *Al Jazeera*, July 1, 2015, at http://www.aljazeera.com/indepth/opinion/2015/06/contest-quasi-states-isil-rojava-150624054713157.html.
37. "The fragile gains of Syria's Kurds", *Stratfor*, July 31, 2015, at https://www.stratfor.com/analysis/fragile-gains-syrias-kurds.
38. Kristian Coates Ulrichsen, "Qatar and the Arab Spring: policy drivers and regional implications", Carnegie Endowment for International Peace, September 24, 2014, at http://carnegieendowment.org/2014/09/24/qatar-and-arab-spring-policy-drivers-and-regional-implications#.
39. Mehran Kamrava, "Mediation and Qatari foreign policy", *Middle East Journal*, 65 (4), Autumn 2011, pp. 539-556.
40. Lina Khatib, "Qatar's foreign policy: the limits of pragmatism", *International Affairs*, 89 (2), 2013, pp. 417-431.
41. "Qatar recognises Libyan rebels after oil deal", *Al Jazeera*, March 28, 2013 at http://www.aljazeera.com/news/middleeast/2011/03/2011328144 50241767.html
42. "Qatar sends fighter jets to enforce no-fly zone", *The Wall Street Journal*, March 20, 2011, at http://online.wsj.com/article/SB10001424052748704433904576212 852941096150.html
43. "Qatar admits sending hundreds of troops to support Libya rebels", *The Guardian*, October 26, 2011, at http://www.guardian.co.uk/world/2011/oct/26/qatar-troops-libya-rebels-support
44. "Arab states arm rebels as UN talks of Syrian civil war", *The Independent*, June 13, 2012, at http://www.independent.co.uk/news/world/middle-east/exclusive-arab-states-arm-rebels-as-un-talks-of-syrian-civil-war-7845026.html
45. "Getting closer to Qatar", *Al Ahram Weekly*, Issue No.1130, January 10, 2013, at http://weekly.ahram.org.eg/News/965/17/Getting-closer-to-Qatar.aspx.
46. "Key excerpts of the Joint Comprehensive Plan of Action (JCPOA)", White House, US, at https://www.whitehouse.gov/sites/default/files/docs/jcpoa_key_excerpts.pdf.
47. Fahimeh Ghorbani, "Iran's relations with Saudi Arabia in post-JCPOA era," *Iran Review*, March 22, 2016, Institute for Middle East Strategic Studies (IMESS), Tehran, at http://en.cmess.ir/Default.aspx?tabid=98&articleid= 654 & dnnprintmode =true&mid= 477&SkinSrc=%5BG%5DSkins%2F_ default%2FNo + Skin&ContainerSrc=%5BG%5DContainers%2F_default%2FNo+Container.
48. James Phillips, "The dangerous regional implications of the Iran nuclear agreement", The Heritage Foundation, May 9, 2016, at http://www.heritage.org/research/reports/2016/05/the-dangerous-regional-implications-of-the-iran-nuclear-agreement#_ftn22.
49. Robert Einhorn and Richard Nephew, "The Iran nuclear deal: prelude to proliferation in the Middle East?" Arms Control and Non-Proliferation Series Paper 11, Brookings Institution, May 2016, at http://www.brookings.edu/~/media/Research/Files/Reports/2016/05/iran-deal-regional-proliferation/The-Iran-Nuclear-Dealwebv4.pdf?la=en.
50. "Saudi Arabia promises to match Iran in nuclear capability", *The New York Times*, May 13, 2015, at http://www.nytimes.com/2015/05/14/world/middleeast/saudi-arabia-promises-to-match-iran-in-nuclear-capability.html.

51. "The Saudis are ready to go nuclear", *The Telegraph* (London), June 8, 2015, at http://www.telegraph.co.uk/news/worldnews/middleeast/saudiarabia/11658338/The-Saudis-are-ready-to-go-nuclear.html.
52. "KSA forms 34-country Islamic military alliance against terror", *Saudi Gazette*, December 16, 2015, at http://saudigazette.com.sa/saudi-arabia/ksa-forms-34-country-islamic-military-alliance-against-terror/.
53. "Led by KSA, 34-nation alliance to wipe out terror", *Arab News*, December 15, 2015, at http://www.arabnews.com/featured/news/850596. The members of the coalition are Bahrain, Bangladesh, Benin, Chad, Comoros, Djibouti, Egypt, Gabon, Guinea, Ivory Coast, Jordan, Kuwait, Lebanon, Libya, Malaysia, Maldives, Mali, Mauritania, Morocco, Niger, Nigeria, Pakistan, Palestine, Qatar, Saudi Arabia, Senegal, Sierra Leone, Somalia, Sudan, Togo, Tunisia, Turkey, UAE and Yemen.
54. Brian Michael Jenkins, "A Saudi-Led Military Alliance to Fight Terrorism", RAND Corporation, 2016, at http://www.rand.org/content/dam/rand/pubs/perspectives/PE100/PE189/RAND_PE189.pdf.
55. Prasanta Kumar Pradhan, "Islamic State and the changing West Asian geopolitics", in S.D. Muni and Vivek Chadha (eds.), *Terrorism: Emerging Trends*, Pentagon Press and IDSA, New Delhi, 2016, p. 107.
56. "20 countries to fire up 'North Thunder'", *Arab News*, February 14, 2016, at http://www.arabnews.com/saudi-arabia/news/880491.
57. "'North Thunder' raised combat readiness: King", *Saudi Gazette*, March 15, 2016, at http://saudigazette.com.sa/saudi-arabia/north-thunder-raised-combat-readiness-king/.
58. "The Saudi message: Operation 'North Thunder' simulates real war", *Asharq Al Awsat*, March 11, 2016, at http://english.aawsat.com/2016/03/article55348383/the-saudi-message-operation-north-thunder-simulates-real-war.
59. "Arab League approves Syria sanctions", *Al Jazeera*, November 28, 2011, at http://www.aljazeera.com/news/middleeast/2011/11/20111127143750187116.html.
60. "Arab League Chief calls on members to confront the Islamic State", *The Huffington Post*, September 8, 2014, at http://www.huffingtonpost.com/2014/09/07/isis-arab-league_n_5780508.html?ir=India&adsSiteOverride=in.
61. "Arab League: ISIS destruction of Iraqi heritage 'odious crime'", *Al Arabiya*, February 27, 2015, at http://english.alarabiya.net/en/News/middle-east/2015/02/27/Arab-League-ISIS-destruction-of-Iraqi-heritage-odious-crime-.html.
62. "Arab League vows military support for Libya, no word on air strikes", *Reuters*, August 18, 2015, at http://www.reuters.com/article/2015/08/18/us-libya-security-idUSKCN0QN1R420150818.
63. "Arab League leaders agree joint military force", *Al Arabiya*, March 29, 2015, at http://english.alarabiya.net/en/News/middle-east/2015/03/29/Arab-League-Summit-.html.
64. "Egypt FM: Arab League close to forming joint military force", *Asharq Al-Awsat*, May 9, 2014, at http://www.aawsat.net/2015/05/article55343360/egypt-fm-arab-league-close-to-forming-jointmilitary-force.
65. "Iraq steps up anti-Daesh coordination with Iran, Syria, Russia", *Khaleej Times*, September 27, 2015, at http://www.khaleejtimes.com/region/mena/iraq-steps-up-anti-daesh-coordination-with-iran-syria-russia.

66. "Some 2,400 Russians fighting for ISIL – Russian FSB", *News.Az*, September 18, 2015, at http://www.news.az/articles/russia/101259.
67. "Ayatollah Khamenei condemns Saudi execution of Sheikh Nimr", Statement by Ayatollah Khamenei on January 3, 2016, at http://english.khamenei.ir/news/3023/Ayatollah-Khamenei-condemns-Saudi-execution-of-Sheikh-Nimr.
68. "Saudi Arabia cuts ties with Iran, expels Tehran envoys", *Saudi Gazette*, January 4, 2016, at http://saudigazette.com.sa/saudi-arabia/saudi-cuts-ties-with-iran-expels-tehran-envoys/.

2

Bahrain: Protests and the Sectarian Politics

Politics, Demography and Sectarianism

Bahrain is an island kingdom in the Gulf with a total population of about 1.3 million[1] with a large number of expatriate workers. Around 70 percent of the native population belongs to the Shia sect and the rest are Sunnis. The Khalifa family belonging to the Sunni sect rules over the island kingdom. In the past, people have protested against the regime demanding freedom, equality and political reforms. The rulers have adopted both coercion and cooption methods to deal with the popular protests. Several opposition political groups and leaders have emerged in recent times with various demands. The issues of corruption and human rights violations have often been highlighted by the opposition leaders most of whom belong to the Shia community. In the 1980s and 1990s, there were periodic eruptions of Shia protests in the country against the regime, occasionally setting off small bombs as well. Also, the Shias have on a number of occasions carried pictures of Ayatollah Khomeini and Ayatollah Khamenei in their *Ashura* processions, representing their symbolic allegiance to the Iranian leaders.[2] Protests and demonstrations by the people creates nervousness for the regime but the Shias showing allegiance to the Iranian leader Khomeini has become a red line for the regime.

Since the discovery of oil, Bahrain has become a leading financial and business hub in the region with a flourishing industry, banking and other infrastructure sectors. Distribution of revenue is a major function of the state, but allegations of unequal distribution of revenues prevail which is a major reason for domestic discontent in Bahrain. Often political and economic bargains have taken place between the government and the opposition. The opposition criticises the government for its excessive dependence on oil revenues, and at the same time, the opposition wants to have a say in the decision making of allotment of oil revenues. The opposition has often complained of discrimination in the allotment of oil revenues against the Shia community. Therefore, one of the main demands of the opposition is to end the discrimination in this regard.[3] Economic discrimination by the state on the basis of loyalty to the regime has been one of the factors giving rise to sectarian politics in the country.

The demographic composition (Shia majority and Sunni minority) of the country does not favour the ruling Al Khalifa family. The opposition groups allege that the Khalifas are trying to alter the demographic balance by providing citizenship to Sunnis from other countries. They are being called as the 'politically naturalised' citizens mostly hailing from countries like Saudi Arabia, Syria, Yemen, Jordan, and Pakistan. To further dismay of the opposition and the dissidents, most of these politically naturalised citizens are employed in the military and security services by the government. This has led the opposition to believe that they have been given Bahraini citizenship to control the local population majority of whom are Shias. This has created anxiety among the opposition, which they strongly believe is a deliberate attempt to change the demography and creating a demographic imbalance in the country. It is estimated that there are around 50,000 to 200,000 foreigners who have been given such citizenship by the ruling family.[4] The opposition Al Wefaq (officially known as Al Wefaq National Islamic Society), citing data obtained from the state-run Central Information Organisation, claimed in August 2014 that 95,372 foreigners have been granted Bahraini citizenship, thereby adding 17.3 per cent to the total population. Al Wefaq believes that this pace of naturalisation in Bahrain poses a serious threat to its society and economy; and by 2040 that will make Bahrainis a minority in their own country. For Al Wefaq, naturalisation is a crime as it harms both Sunnis and Shias in the country. It believes that the government is making a mistake by believing that naturalisation would help it in future. Rather it will create more problems for the future government, as it will be facing a new set of problems when the Bahrainis become a minority.[5] While the discontent over demographic change continues among the opposition, the regime still persists with its policy of naturalising Sunnis from other countries as its citizens.

For a long time, the Shias have alleged political, economic and social discrimination by the government. Much before the present king Sheikh Hamad came to power in 1999, they repeatedly presented petitions to his father Sheikh Isa bin Salman, demanding reform in the country. Unemployment rate among the Shias in Bahrain is disproportionately high compared to the Sunnis. They are also not proportionally represented in the higher ranks of military, police and civil service. Many of the Shias have complained of their poor economic conditions as compared to the Sunnis. But despite such allegations and demands of the people Sheikh Isa took no meaningful action. Parliament, which was the only forum available for the opposition leaders to raise their concerns, remained suspended for decades. On the other hand, opposition figures were targeted by the regime. While some of them were jailed and many others fled the country. Such crackdown on the opposition leaders took away temporary pressure for reform off the King, but the dissatisfaction among the Shia majority towards the regime continued to simmer endlessly.

King Hamad, after coming to power in 1999 and witnessing a number of popular uprisings, introduced some political reforms. He repealed the emergency laws prevailing for the past 25 years and released a large number of political prisoners. A number of dissident political leaders were also allowed to return to the country. The National Action Charter was approved in a nation-wide referendum in 2001. This has been regarded as an important step forward in the direction of reforms and political development in the kingdom. The following year, in 2002, a new constitution was promulgated. Among other things, the constitution officially converted the country from an 'emirate' to a 'constitutional monarchy', created a bicameral legislature, called for equality between the Shias and Sunnis, provided civil rights to the citizens and allowed women to participate in the political process in the country. After initiating such reforms, Hamad then declared himself as the 'king' in 2002.

A major barrier to the functioning of the parliament has been sectarian politics in the kingdom. In the first parliament of 1972, 16 out of the 30 members were Shias. The Khalifa family suspended the parliament when it did not approve a restrictive law.[6] The opposition in the new parliament of 2002 has challenged the regime as well. Election boycott by Al Wefaq reduced the number of Shia representatives in parliament, but it has remained an avenue for expressing their opinion before the government.

Popular Protests

In Bahrain, popular protests against the regime started in February 2011. The protesters, who gathered at the famous Pearl Roundabout in the capital city of Manama, demanded political reforms, social equality and economic well-being. Most of the protesters were educated young men and women who had their own aspirations to participate in the affairs of the country. The protesters used the internet and social networking sites to spread their messages and thereby were able to gather more people to put forward their demands. On February 14, 2011, the protesters declared 'Day of Rage', the Egypt-style mass congregation of demonstrators, gathering at the Pearl Roundabout. February 14 bears an important symbolic value for the opposition in Bahrain, as it was on the same day Bahraini people won a referendum by around 98 per cent of the votes in 2001 in favour of the National Action Charter.[7] So it was a day of historical significance for the Bahrainis. The call for the 'Day of Rage' gathered thousands of people who camped at the Pearl Roundabout in Manama. Such a huge gathering accelerated their demands for reform and put direct pressure on the regime to respond.

Opposing these protests, some pro-regime groups demonstrated in support of the government. These groups constituted mostly Sunnis who are loyal to the regime. There were also reports of involvement of many pro-regime criminal elements among the Sunni demonstrators who allegedly attacked the Shia protesters. For the pro-regime Sunnis, the demands of political reform by the majority Shias were a direct attack on the Sunni identity of the kingdom. They also believed that showing greater leniency towards the Shias during protests may look as 'a sign of weakness of the regime' and that maintaining status quo was thought to be more important than granting political liberties to the Shias.[8] This aroused the sectarian sentiments among the Shias, who initially claimed their protests to be peaceful.

The government responded with a heavy hand, which involved several deaths and imprisonment of the protesters. There were also reports of torture in custody of opposition leaders and dissidents. Prominent opposition figure Sheikh Ali Salman and human rights activist Nabeel Rajab were also jailed. Others arrested included doctors, journalists, lawyers and intellectuals. The government also revoked the citizenship of a number of people.[9] The government then invited the Gulf Cooperation Council (GCC) on March 14 seeking military help from the neighbours. It declared a 'State of National Security',[10] giving wide-ranging authority to the military chief, and began a crackdown against the protestors at the Pearl Roundabout, but the protests continued on the streets.

Role of the Opposition

During the protests, Al Wefaq played an important role in bringing people together. Political parties are banned in Bahrain and are therefore called 'political societies'. Al Wefaq's political support comes mainly from the Shias and it is the largest political group in the country. It has been fighting for political and legislative power for the people. Many of the leaders of Al Wefaq were exiled following the nation-wide popular unrest in 1990s demanding democratic reforms including reinstatement of the parliament, which was earlier dissolved by the King. Despite the political reforms initiated by King Hamad, differences in the approach of King and Al Wefaq continued. King Hamad has been reluctant to let go of power. On the other hand, Al Wefaq wanted fundamental political re-orientation in the country, which would provide it more political and legislative power and would undermine the powers of the King.[11] It participated in the national dialogue initiated by the king and later withdrew alleging lack of seriousness of the government towards the dialogue. In October 2014, a court in Bahrain banned Al Wefaq for three months in response to a suit filed by the Justice Ministry, which alleged that the group was breaking the law. It asked Al Wefaq to rectify its 'illegal status following the annulment of four general assemblies for lack of a quorum and non-commitment to the public and transparency requirements for holding them.'[12] But the group still remains active and vocal.

Earlier on July 2, 2011, the government proposed a national reconciliation process with the opposition groups. The latter also nominated some members for the talks. But on July 17, Al Wefaq withdrew from the talks, stating that the government was lacking seriousness to go ahead with the process of national reconciliation talks with the opposition groups. Al Wefaq then reiterated its demands for the establishment of democratic institutions in the country and beginning of the process towards democratic reforms. It demanded an elected government, an elected parliament with full legislative powers and a fair and independent judicial system in the country. Al Wefaq has always stated that any government in the country should be based on the legitimacy given by the country's people.[13] Al Wefaq's leader Sheikh Ali Salman said in a speech on February 25, 2011 at the Pearl Roundabout:

> "We don't want a religious state. We want a state where the people elect their government. Our demand is freedom and democracy, not a religious or sectarian state. Everybody is demanding a civil, democratic and tolerant state coherent with its region and the Gulf Council and the Arab world as Bahrain always lived in peace and harmony."[14]

This very claim makes the regime nervous as it runs contrary to the nature of governance of the Khalifa family. The demands for a democratic system of governance directly threatens the ruling family as it would loosen their exclusive hold on power in the country and their legitimacy will be put at stake.

The Waad (National Democratic Action Society) is the second-largest Shia-dominated opposition political society in Bahrain. It was banned in April 2011 amidst the increasing protests in the country. After the government proposed holding the national dialogue, the ban on the Waad was lifted and it was invited to participate in the dialogue. Its Secretary General Ibrahim Sharif was arrested in 2011, released in 2015, and rearrested the following month. The Waad demands a state with freedom, democracy and social justice and which respects human rights and embodies equal citizenship without discrimination or marginalisation.[15] Like the demands put forward by Al Wefaq, Waad's political demands are also difficult for the royal family to accept as it will gradually make them irrelevant and powerless.

Response of the State

The response of the regime to the protests was characteristic of an authoritarian state. Disproportionate military response and unjustified political decisions were key features of the regime's response to the protests. The regime used excessive force on the protesters and tried to disperse the protesters from the Pearl Roundabout which was the epicentre of the protests. Security forces were deployed in large numbers after the protesters gave a call for the Day of Rage throughout the country on February 14, 2011. There were reports of heavily armed riot police using tear gas, rubber bullets and live ammunition to disperse the protesters in many places. A number of protesters were killed by the security forces and a large number of them were injured. The use of force to control the protests drew sharp criticism not only from the domestic opposition but also internationally. As the protests gathered more strength, on February 17, 2011, the security forces took control of the Pearl Roundabout. The excessive use of force was visible in Manama where the regime used tanks and helicopters to control the situation.

But in a move for appeasement, on February 19, 2011 the government announced a national mourning for those killed during the protests, describing them as the 'sons we have lost'.[16] Three days later, King Hamad offered to release a number of prisoners, including 25 Shias.[17] Further, five days later, King Hamad dismissed three of his ministers.[18] But the protesters continued with their protests. The government then offered to begin a process of negotiation with the protesters and invited various political societies, business leaders and societal figures for consultation. Crown Prince Salman led the consultation process from the government side. A statement was then released on March 13, 2011, which identified seven important principles on which the national dialogue should focus, as follows: (1) a parliament with full authority; (2) a government that represents the will of the people; (3) naturalisation; (4) fair voting districts; (5) combating corruption; (6) state property; and (7) addressing sectarian tension. But with the situation changing rapidly, the opposition placed other demands such as election of a Constituent Assembly to rewrite the constitution and put preconditions to join the national dialogue, which included the resignation of the Prime Minister and the government.[19]

Meanwhile, the government's security crackdown and political offensive continued. Several opposition leaders and activists were jailed, including Hassan Mushaima and Abdul Jalil Al Singace, leaders of the Haq movement; Ibrahim Sharif, head of the Waad; Abdul Wahad Hussein of Al Wafa Islamic Movement; and Hassan Hadad and Abdul Hadi Al Mokhdar.[20] With the continuing protests and increasing violence, the government banned all protests and political gatherings. Soon thereafter, on March 14, the GCC forces under the Peninsula Shield Force entered Bahrain at King Hamad's request. The next day, the government declared a three-month state of emergency, because it believed that there was 'increased lawlessness jeopardising the lives of citizens and resulting in the violation of private property, disruption of livelihoods and extending to the damage of state institutions.'[21]

The regime's strategy to deal with the protests was primarily military-centric. Even after the temporary pause in the protests and violence, according to Al Wefaq, in 2015 alone the government arrested 1765 people, including 120 children. Between 2012 and 2015, the government also revoked the Bahraini citizenship of 260 people, most of whom are political activists, human rights activists and journalists, accusing them of 'harming the interests of the kingdom' or acting 'contrary to the duty of loyalty'.[22] Human rights activists have been targeted by the government. Prominent Bahraini Human rights activists such as Nabeel Rajab, Maryam Al Khawaja, her sister Zainab

Al Khawaja have been arrested for several fictitious reasons. Abdulhadi Al Khawaja, the father of Maryam and Zainab, was arrested during the protests in 2011 and is serving a life term in prison now. Some prominent political opposition figures such as Sheikh Ali Salman, Secretary General of Al Wefaq, Ebrahim Sharif of the Waad party and Fadhel Abbas Mahdi Mohamed, Secretary General of Al Wahdawy party have been arrested and jailed by the authorities. Such crackdown by the government dilutes its efforts of political negotiation and dialogue with the opposition. As most of the opposition, human rights activists and protesters belong to the Shia community, an obvious sectarian sentiment tends to dominate the whole discourse of protests and political developments Bahrain. The state has used all the political and security apparatuses available at its hand to suppress the opposition. When the legitimacy of an authoritarian state is questioned by its own majority population, then response of the regime to such a crisis, expectedly, has become coercive.

Laurence Louer notes that though the majority of the Bahraini population is Shia, the security establishments are dominated by the Sunnis in a 'coup proofing strategy' by the regime, which perceives the Shias to be intrinsically untrustworthy.[23] Bahrain's military forces also come from tribal connections and are overwhelmingly controlled by the Khalifa family. In this patrimonial system, the large number of foreigners present in the military are 'largely detached from the local population',[24] which naturally creates dissension among the Shia population. The fact that there are a large number of foreigners in the security forces has led some scholars to criticise by saying that the Bahraini army is 'not a national army'; rather, it can be called as a 'fighting force of Sunni Muslims who are charged with protecting a Sunni ruling family and Sunni political and business elites in a country.'[25] The sectarian politics in Bahrain combined with the nature of the composition of the military forces and their role during the protests remain contentious today.

National Dialogue: The Regime's Reconciliation Move

To pacify the protesters, the government announced to hold a national dialogue in the country inviting all the major stakeholders to participate and discuss the important issues concerning them. In the face of severe protests and the criticism of government's crackdown on the protesters, in a seemingly conciliatory move, the king offered a national dialogue indicating his willingness to initiate reforms and to engage with the people. King Hamad appointed Parliament's Speaker Khalifa bin Ahmed Al Dhahrani to chair the National Dialogue. The invitees numbered 300 members from government, opposition political groups, civil society and media. The dialogue was to begin on July 2, 2011 to deliberate on four important themes – political, economic, social and legal – with the slogan "Our Bahrain, Our Unity". Each invited group was to have five representatives.

The government made all possible efforts at its disposal to encourage participation in the dialogue. The government expressed its seriousness about the possible outcome of the dialogue. In order to instil optimism and encourage participation of the opposition in the dialogue, King Hamad said that "all the options are on the table" for the dialogue. He also assured the opposition by saying that "it will be a true dialogue in every respect and no section of the Bahrain's wide a diverse society will be ignored."[26] Similarly, Isa Abdulrahman, the spokesman for the National dialogue, expressed his optimism and said that the dialogue "offered an opportunity for reform while easing tensions between the country's majority Shias and minority Sunnis".[27] He stated that the "aim of the National Dialogue was to reach a consensus on a wider range of issues of concern to the Bahraini people. From the government's narrative, "the dialogue aims at bringing together the various segments of the Bahraini society to present people's views and demands for further reform in the country without any preconditions and with the consensus of all participants."[28] But the opposition had their own scepticism regarding the intention of the regime. A major cause of concern for the opposition to join the dialogue was the number of seats allocated to them was much less than what they expected. Out of the total 300 members of the dialogue, only 35 seats were given to the opposition groups. The main opposition party Al Wefaq initially refused to participate but was persuaded by the regime for the national dialogue. Al Wefaq believed that national dialogue is an eyewash by the regime who is not serious to address the genuine demands of the people and it is only another ploy by the regime to continue with their policy of discrimination. But later it agreed to join the dialogue after being convinced by the government. Its leader Sheikh Ali Salman stated that Al Wefaq would join the dialogue but "if the dialogue does not deliver what the people need, we will withdraw."[29] Thus, clearly Al Wefaq set the precondition before joining the dialogue. Two weeks after the National dialogue began, on July 17, 2011, Al Wefaq pulled out, of the dialogue alleging that the talks were 'not serious' and were exploitative of its goodwill, and that they do not help find a 'political solution' for Bahrain's problems. Al Wefaq stated that, "we feel that our participation is being taken advantage of in order to distort the meaning of national dialogue and national consensus.... This will exacerbate the political impasse and our presence is being used to pass pre-planned results."[30] Al Wefaq also complained that though it had won 64 per cent of votes in the previous last elections, it was allowed only five representatives in the dialogue.[31] The National dialogue was then temporarily suspended in July 2011. It was resumed in February 2013 to complete the mission on building consensus among the people. But it had to be suspended as Al Wefaq again withdrew from the resumed dialogue after one of its party leaders, Khalil Marzook, was arrested in September 2013 on the charges of inciting violence and terrorism. This led to sharp reactions from Al Wefaq who alleged that the government is targeting the political opposition and escalating further tension in the country.[32] This time it was not only Al Wefaq, rather the opposition coalition called as the National Democratic Opposition Parties (NDOP) withdrew from the dialogue. The NDOP comprises Al Wefaq National Islamic Society (Al Wefaq), Al National Democratic Action Society (Waad), National Democratic Gathering Society (Al Qawmi), Al Wahdawy (Unitary National Democratic Assemblage) and Ekhaa National Society (Ekhaa). In September 2013, the NDOP objected to an order by the Minister of Justice and Islamic Affairs, which required "a representative of the Ministry of Foreign Affairs or the Government be present in meetings between political societies and diplomatic missions, foreign embassies in Bahrain and governmental organisations and representatives of foreign states."[33] The government order required the opposition to take its prior approval before meeting any foreign embassy officials, which the opposition viewed as expressing the government's scepticism over its patriotism.[34] Both the government and the opposition remained adamant in their positions and the national dialogue process was suspended in January 2014.

Thus, the national dialogue process suffered and was once again stalled midway without reaching any consensus among the parties. This reflected deep divisions between the regime and the opposition over the important political, economic and security issues. While the regime remained stubborn over giving more freedom, human rights and reforming the system, the opposition became more vocal in airing their views to the government. The government's crackdown on some political leaders has not discouraged the opposition. Rather the non-serious allegations on them such as inciting terrorism, violence, attempts to overthrow the regime etc. weaken the charges made by the government. As of now the National Dialogue process remains suspended. Though there are reports of attempts by the regime to bring the opposition back to the dialogue table, a lot would depend upon the ability and seriousness of the government to engage with the opposition.

Bahrain Independent Commission of Inquiry (BICI)

Meanwhile, the government appointed an independent commission of enquiry in July 2011 to investigate the incidents that took place during the protests of February-March that year and to suggest appropriate recommendations. This was indeed an unprecedented step on the part of an authoritarian regime. The five-member commission headed by the Egyptian-American lawyer Cherif Bassiouni, with Nigel Rodley, Badria Al-Awadhi, Philippe Kirsch and Mahnoush H. Arsanjani as members.[35] The commission submitted a 513-page report in November 2011. It noted that the security forces entered homes and arrested people without producing an arrest warrant, which 'involved unnecessary excessive force, accompanied by terror-inspiring behaviour'.[36] It found that the Bahraini security forces which entered homes to search and arrest people were indulged in sectarian insults, verbal abuses and humiliated women as well. The commission also found 'disregard for Bahrain law and international human rights law pertaining to fairness and due process in connection with arrests.' It also expressed the belief that such arrests could not have been possible without the knowledge of the higher commands of the Ministry of Interior (MoI) and the National Security Agency (NSA). A large number of detainees were subjected to "mistreatment, including torture and other forms of cruel, inhuman or degrading treatment."[37] This kind of physical and psychological treatment was intended to extract confessions or as retribution or punishment. Also, the "NSA and MoI followed a systematic practice of physical and psychological mistreatment, which in many cases amounted to torture, with respect to a large number of detainees in their custody."[38] A large number of Shia mosques were demolished during that period by MoI's Department of General Security and Department of Riot Police.

The BICI's recommendations included:[39] (i) establishing an impartial national commission to follow up on its recommendations; (ii) changes in the structure and functioning of the office of the Inspector General and the NSA; (iii) investigating into the killings by the security forces, punishment for those found guilty, compensation for the victims, and establishing an independent enquiry committee to look into the matters of torture, abuses and the excessive use of force by the authorities; (iv) following up on the King's announcement that new Shiite mosques would be built and rebuilding some of the Shia religious structures which were damaged during the protests; (v) running educational programmes in educational institutions which would encourage tolerance, human rights and rule of law; and (vi) relaxing censorship on the print and electronic media.

The opposition groups have appreciated the findings of the report but, at the same time, they have alleged that the government has not implemented the majority of these recommendations made by the BICI.[40] Even criticism of government's implementation of the BICI recommendations came from none other than Cherif Bassiouni, the head of the BICI, has confirmed this view. In an interview in June 2014, Bassiouni stated that though the Bahraini government has 'consistently carried out the implementation of the recommendations', those were being made on a 'piecemeal level', and thus are losing its 'cumulative impact.'[41] International human rights organisations like Amnesty

International and Human Rights Watch have also severely criticised the government's failure to implement the BICI recommendation.

Saudi Arabia and Protests in Bahrain

The kingdoms of Saudi Arabia and Bahrain enjoy a close neighbourly relationship. The ruling family of both the countries maintain close relationship with each other. The Khalifa family of Bahrain came to power in the eighteenth century by defeating the Persians with the help of the rulers of the Arabian Peninsula. Currently, both the Saudi and Bahraini kingdoms are members of the GCC and share similar views on a large number of regional political, economic and security-related issues. Although there are several differences among some members of the GCC, the Saudi-Bahraini ties remain strong. Riyadh has been challenged, on several issues, by Qatar and Oman. While Qatar maintains its own regional ambitions, Oman intends to maintain a neutral foreign policy in these turbulent times. Bahrain, however, remains a trusted ally of Saudi Arabia.

Bahrain's geographical location is important for Saudi Arabia from a geostrategic point of view. Saudi Arabia is the biggest Arab neighbour, with strong political, economic and strategic links. The King Fahd Causeway, which connects the two nations and has been funded by Saudi Arabia, is the only land link between them. The Causeway was opened for public in 1986. In February 2016 the two countries announced that the causeway would be expanded from the existing 17 lanes to 45 lanes, and the work would start in six months' time.[42] Besides facilitating trade and connectivity between the two countries, the Causeway has been a useful instrument for Saudi Arabia to check any security threat emanating from Bahrain. Beyond the proximity between the two kingdoms, the geopolitical consideration of Iranian intervention in Bahrain is also important for both Bahrain and Saudi Arabia. For Riyadh, the stability of the Khalifa regime in Manama is necessary to prevent increasing Iranian involvement in the island kingdom.[43] Saudi Arabia considers Bahrain to be its traditional sphere of influence and believes that some sections of the Bahraini Shias have close links with Iran.

Saudi Arabia has extensive political and strategic interests in

Bahrain. As the political protests began in Bahrain, Saudi Arabia's major concern was the possible spread of protests to its own territory, especially among its Shia majority in its Eastern Province. Much like the tribal links between the two royal families, the Shias in Bahrain also possess strong ties with the Shias in Saudi Arabia. The Saudi Shias are also alleged to have religious connections with the Shias in Iran and are often perceived as Iran's fifth column.[44] Saudi Arabia has in the past witnessed protests by its Shia minority, constituting around 10-15 percent its population demanding political reforms, religious freedom and economic equality. The Eastern Province, which has been regularly discriminated against by the Al Saud regime, remains its Achilles' heel.[45] The Shias face pervasive political discrimination in the country and are studiously excluded from the mainstream politics. There is no Shiite representation at the upper echelons of Saudi government. They are only marginally represented in the judiciary, military, security forces, and the National Guard. The huge oil revenues acquired by the government have not been shared fairly with Shia communities. While the towns of Damman and Khobar have grown into flourishing industrial centres, the Shia-populated neighbouring settlements of Qatif and Hufuf have been left behind.

After the success of the Islamic Revolution in Iran in 1979, in 1980 the Saudi Shias organised demonstrations and a series of strikes to celebrate it. The government repressed this event in a ham-handed way, leading to many deaths. The Shias remember the events as 'the uprising of the Eastern province', a symbol of repression to which the community has historically been subjected.[46] In the mid-1970s and early 1980s, Shia opposition was always critical of the government and the Shias openly criticised the state and denounced its discriminatory policies. The Shia opposition has considered the Saud regime as illegitimate.[47] The Shia resistance has manifested itself in various ways, ranging from letters to princes, petitions to local governors, and open confrontation with the government in demonstrations.[48] But in recent decades the regime has tried to restrain itself in its discrimination against the Shias. The Saudi Shias also have found ways to put forward their demands peacefully. But despite that the issue still remains critical for the regime and the Saudi royal family remains apprehensive about the internal security threat involving the Shias in the Eastern Province.

Nevertheless, the Saudi royal family has in the past alleged that some members of the kingdom's Shia community maintain links with their coreligionists outside the kingdom. The Saudi regime does not favour any democratic reforms such as what the protesters in Bahrain were demanding. It also does not support any negotiations with the protesters, seeing it as the thin edge of a wedge. Also, an elected parliament would lead to a majority of Shia members being elected as members of parliament. This would in turn lead to Iranian dominance, as is the case of Iraq.[49] The International Crisis Group states that 'Saudi Arabia purportedly is responding to dual fears: that the popular uprising could lead to a Shiite takeover, and a Shiite takeover would be tantamount to an Iranian one.'[50] In this regard, it fears contamination from a Shia-influenced politics from Bahrain.

Bahrain is also important from a regional military and strategic viewpoint in the Gulf region. The US Navy's Fifth Fleet is located in Bahrain. The US military presence is necessary for Saudi Arabia to ensure smooth flow of oil in the Gulf waters. Unhindered supply of oil is the lifeline of the economy of the region, and thus, any disturbance in Bahrain has the potential to shake the international oil market.[51] Saudi Arabia prefers a stable oil market, with oil at reasonable prices. The Saudi rulers believe that any disturbances in the international oil market would disturb its buyers. Though a steep rise in oil prices may provide it immediate monetary gains, in the long term its buyers may look for alternate sources for their energy needs.[52] Therefore, it was important to maintain peace and stability in the region. In this manner, the protests in Bahrain were a potential indirect challenge for the Saudi economy.

Bahrain came as the most direct challenge for Saudi security and foreign policy in the region. Both geographical and demographic dimensions of the conflict in Bahrain were the immediate triggers for Saudi Arabia to militarily intervene in Bahrain to help the Khalifa regime ward off any threats to their regime security. Saudi Arabia claims that the GCC forces were not engaged in confronting the protesters and were deployed to protect the strategic infrastructure such as refineries, airport, seaport and economic installations, it certainly helped the Bahraini authorities to put down the protests.[53]

GCC Support for the Khalifa Regime

In the midst of severe protests by the people, the Khalifa regime got unwavering support from the GCC. Like Saudi Arabia, the other GCC leaders also believed that the protests in Bahrain could lead to Iran exploiting the situation to its advantage. Their apprehension was that Iran was using the cover of the uprisings in Egypt and Libya to weaken the Khalifa family's grip on power in Bahrain and to replicate the phenomenon elsewhere in the Gulf.[54] Rejecting external interference in Bahrain's internal matters, the GCC's Ministerial Council (comprising of Foreign Ministers) said that "it would face with firmness and decisiveness whoever tried to tamper with their security and interests or spread the seeds of rift and sedition among their peoples." It also expressed solidarity with the Khalifa regime and "considered any harm to the security of any of its members as detrimental to all members alike, triggering decisive and firm unhesitant response."[55] Such unwavering support was later exhibited in the form of military support by the GCC Peninsula Shield Force in Bahrain was crucial for the survival of the Khalifa regime. The leaders of the GCC have repeatedly expressed their opinion standing with the Bahrain royal family. According to Brandon Friedman,

> "Statements throughout April and May 2011 from key GCC officials suggest that they feel that Iran will exploit any weakness in the Gulf regimes to promote Shiite ascendancy and increase its power at the expense of the Sunni rulers in the region. The monarchies see Iran as attempting to turn the Arab uprisings into another Iranian revolution."[56]

The GCC statement in this regard emphasised their position as:

> "The GCC States have asserted that they will stand by each other in case of any danger posed to any Member State. They also have asserted their full support to the Kingdom of Bahrain on political, economic, security and defence fronts, following the events of February and March 2011, based on the principle of preserving collective, integrated and interdependent security and considering the security and stability of the GCC States as an integral whole, and out of their commitment to the pledges and common security and defence agreements and not accepting intervention of any external party in the affairs of the Kingdom of Bahrain."[57]

The GCC leaders felt that Iran may exploit the situation to its favour using its Shiite connection and saw it as an Iranian attempt to turn the protests in Bahrain into another Iranian revolution.[58] The mutual threat perception of an immensely active Iran capitalising the situation in Bahrain brought the GCC countries further closer against Iran. The developments in Bahrain created a domino effect in the region which alarmed the GCC leaders. Besides Bahrain, violent protests against the regime took place in Oman as well. The protests began as small demonstrations by people demanding better wages, better employment opportunities, checking corruption, and so on. Gradually, the demands covered political issues such as demands for political reforms and freedom of expression. Strong protests were witnessed in places like Sohar, Dhofar, Muscat, Haima and Salalah. The protests in Oman were less violent than in other countries such as Egypt, Libya or Bahrain, and the rulers managed the deal with the situation. Sultan Qaboos adopted some measures, which included a cabinet reshuffle, stipends for students, pledging to create 50,000 government jobs, benefits for the unemployed, etc. But the protests in Oman along with the worsening situation in Bahrain certainly worried the GCC about the internal security situation in the region. Oman and Bahrain are relatively weaker economies among the oil-rich countries of the GCC. Therefore, showing strong support with the neighbours facing anti-government protests, in March 2011, GCC announced the establishment of the GCC Developmental Programme (GCCDP) and appropriated an aid package of US$ 20 billion to give US$ 10 billion each to Oman and Bahrain.[59]

Besides the military intervention and the economic aid, the GCC also supported the regime's political initiatives in Bahrain. The GCC also strongly supported the National Dialogue in Bahrain called by the king. GCC Secretary General Abdullatif bin Rashid Al Zayani described the national dialogue as 'a patriotic initiative aimed at addressing the situation in the aftermath of the regrettable events'[60] which took place in February and March 2011. Appreciating the initiative he further stated that 'the national dialogue reflects King Hamad's farsightedness and resolved to continue the march of development and reform towards achieving people's aspirations to a secure and stable life and a better future.'[61] The political, military and financial support provided by the GCC as an organisation was crucial for the Khalifa regime to manage the crisis. An unfriendly attitude from the neighbouring GCC countries would have had devastating results for the ruling family.

Iran and the Protests in Bahrain

Iran openly supported the protesters in Bahrain against the regime. Grand Ayatollah Sayyid Ali Hosseini Khamenei was critical of the Khalifa family and accused it of suppressing the voice of the people. He stated: 'The Islamic Republic of Iran, the nation, government and political elites cannot remain indifferent to the current developments in the region.'[62] He even stated that 'It is the legitimate right of people in Bahrain to express their protest...The government in Bahrain has adopted a wrong approach in dealing with its people and 'the anger of the people may bring down the government in Bahrain.' Khamenei was critical of Saudi Arabia and other GCC countries' role in the matter as they sent their military forces to help Bahrain suppress the protests. Khamenei stated: 'Those who have dispatched military forces to Bahrain have committed a grave mistake.'[63] There was also severe condemnation from the Iranian parliament members regarding the situation in Bahrain. Iran portrayed the protests in Bahrain as domestic in origin which is driven by the desires of the people for political reform.[64] The National Security and Foreign Policy Committee of the Iranian Parliament issued a statement saying, 'The oppressed people of Bahrain are a part of the Islamic world and the Islamic Republic of Iran feels obligated to support them.' The statement called on Saudi Arabia and the UAE to withdraw their forces from Bahrain and alleged the US of attacking Bahrain by using 'regional mercenaries'.[65] Iran further tried to internationalise the Bahrain issue and highlight the oppression of the Bahraini people by the ruling regime and the GCC forces. Iranian Parliament Speaker Ali Larijani called for an emergency conference to be hosted by the Parliamentary Union of the Organisation of Islamic Cooperation (OIC) member states and an emergency meeting by the Asian Parliamentary Assembly (APA).[66] Thousands of Iranians also marched in Tehran in support of the Bahraini protestors.[67]

The Bahrain government has repeatedly rejected the Iranian 'interference in Bahrain'. In February 2016, Interior Minister Shaikh Rashid bin Abdullah Al Khalifa gave a detailed analysis of the Iranian interference in Bahrain's internal security situation. He said:

> "Since 2011, Iran has tried to exploit Bahrain's politics, economy and social fabric to achieve its expansion purposes. They have targeted the security and stability of the nation with weapons and explosives shipments. They have also attempted to destabilise the government and harm the economy. There are terrorist groups in Bahrain that have received training in Iran, Iraq and Syria and that are linked to the Iranian Revolutionary Guard and Hezbollah. Iran offers financial support, weapons and explosives that are smuggled into the country. This includes training in bomb making that has led to the death and injury of several policemen."[68]

He added that Iran was making attempts to disrupt Bahraini national unity by 'igniting sectarian extremism to create sedition between Sunni and Shiite citizens' and 'hindering the political reform process in Bahrain.'[69].

According to the report of the BICI, the Government of Bahrain alleged Iranian involvement in Bahrain's domestic affairs since the Islamic Revolution in 1979. The report noted that the Bahraini government feared an Iranian armed intervention in the country and also asserted that Iranian officials posted in the embassy in Manama contacted opposition leaders during the protests encouraging them to continue their protests and escalate their demands. Similarly, The Khalifa regime also claimed that some of the opposition leaders were in contact with the Hezbollah, asking it to provide training to their followers. But the committee found that the evidence produced by the regime did not 'establish a discernible link between specific incidents that occurred in Bahrain during February and March 2011' and Iran's involvement.[70] Iran's support for the protesters and the opposition is only a complicating factor, as Iran does not have any significant influence in the kingdom. Bahraini Shias do not look to Iran for any religious guidance; the Iraqi religious establishment has more influence over them. Bahraini Shias also do not support the *vilayat e faqih* system of rule. But Bahraini rulers still are wary of Iranian intervention, as some sections in Iran have time and again claimed Bahrain to be an

Iranian province. The sudden increase of Iranian influence in Iraq also adds to Bahraini fears of 'Iranian expansionism'.[71] Amid the allegations and counter-allegations, a higher degree of suspicion and apprehension persists among all the actors – Saudi Arabia, Iran and Bahrain.

In 1981, there was a failed coup attempt in Bahrain allegedly by the Islamic Front for the Liberation of Bahrain (IFLB). Bahraini government claimed that the group was backed by Iran and was inspired by the Islamic Revolution of Iran of 1979. The group intended to overthrow the Khalifa regime and establish an Iranian style Islamic republic in Bahrain.[72] The Bahrain government claimed that the IFLB was trained by the Islamic Revolutionary Guard Corps (IRGC) and received complete support from the Iranian government. This incident largely shaped the regime's suspicion regarding the Shias' patriotism. The regime began to see the Shias as 'intrinsically untrustworthy and liable to act as an Iranian fifth column'.[73] Although there could have been some Bahraini nationals who were involved in the failed coup attempt the regime began to perceive the Shias in general as disloyal to the country. The government used this incident to justify its suspension of the constitution and parliament.[74] The activities of IFLB further consolidated the Bahraini perception about Iranian involvement in their country. For Iran any coup in Bahrain would empower the Shias in the island kingdom and would also embolden Shias of Saudi Arabia.

The Bahraini suspicion about Iranian intervention in the kingdom also flows from the fact that till 1970 Iran claimed Bahrain as part of its territory. The issue first came up in 1930 as the Iranian government protested when the Sheikh of Bahrain granted concession to a British company for exploiting oil resources.[75] Later, the matter became a big issue to be resolved between Iran, Britain and the Sheikh of Bahrain with UN intervention. Iran contended that historically Bahrain had remained under Persian rule except for a small period of Portuguese occupation, thereby challenging the British protectorate over the island. The British held that the Persians were defeated and driven out by the local Arabs, the ancestors of the present Khalifa rulers of Bahrain, in 1783 which marked the end of Persian rule over Bahrain. The Persians asserted that the defeat did not amount to their losing sovereignty nor did it justify Al Khalifa's right to claim sovereignty.[76] It was decided that the issue would be referred to the UN to be resolved. After a lot of deliberations, all the parties – the British, Persian and the Bahraini Emir – agreed to a consultation with the Bahraini people to ascertain their wishes. UN Secretary General U Thant appointed Vittorio Winspeare to Bahrain to consult with the people. In his report to the UN Secretary General, Winspeare stated that the overwhelming majority of the Bahrainis wanted an independent and sovereign state.[77] The Security Council adopted a resolution to this effect unanimously on May 11, 1970. This ended Iran's official claim over Bahrain, but occasional unofficial claims over Bahrain keep flowing from Iran to stoke annoyance for the Bahrain ruling family.

Bahrain's neighbouring Gulf Arab countries like Saudi Arabia and others allege that Iran has connections with the Shias of Bahrain for which they have not been able to provide any substantial evidence to prove their claim. They believe that the religious and sectarian connection is an important link, which draws Iran towards Bahrain. They also believe that Iran intends to utilise that link for its larger strategic interest of creating constituencies throughout the region and to support the opposition to overthrow the Sunni royal families. This would also challenge the legitimacy of the Saud family.[78] Though Iran denies all such allegations of the GCC countries, the mutual suspicion still remains at large. The Bahrain ruling family has often alleged that Iran is trying to exploit the sentiments of some its dissidents and political oppositions.

The US and Protests in Bahrain

As the violence spread in Bahrain, the US expressed its concern regarding peace and stability in the kingdom and urged the Bahrain government 'to take steps to implement reforms and to promote national reconciliation, both through dialogue with political and civil society and through engagement with Bahrain's parliament.'[79] Bahrain is a strategic ally for the US in the Gulf region and a partner in its military initiatives. The US Navy's Fifth Fleet is located in Bahrain. According to Alexander Cooley and Daniel H. Nexon:

> "The Fifth Fleet patrols the Arabian Sea, the Red Sea, the western part of the Indian Ocean, and the Persian Gulf, ensuring that sea-

> lanes remain open, protecting the flow of oil, conducting anti-piracy operations, and acting as a check against Iran's regional influence. Bahrain also hosts the United States' Naval Forces Central Command (NAVCENT) – the maritime component to the US Central Command – and offers US forces the Isa Airbase and space at Bahrain International Airport."[80]

The US designated Bahrain as a major non-NATO ally in 2002.[81] Both the countries signed a Defence Cooperation Agreement earlier in 1991. There are over 8000 US military personnel deployed in Bahrain.[82] When the protests broke out in Bahrain in 2011, the US held up arms sales to Bahrain, suspecting that the weapons might be used by the regime for internal security purposes. In July 2015, the US stated that though the human rights situation in Bahrain was not adequate, there had been some 'meaningful progress on human rights reforms and reconciliation'[83] and lifted the arms embargo.

Because of its military and strategic interests in Bahrain, US reacted with caution to the developments in the kingdom. During the opposition protests in Bahrain, the official US response to the development was cautious. In a statement on February 15, 2011, Philip J. Crowley, the Assistant Secretary of State for Public Affairs, expressed concern about the violence taking place in the country, offered condolences and welcomed the regime's initiative to take legal action against the unjustified use of force.[84] Similarly, after a meeting with Crown Prince Salman on June 7, 2011, Hillary Clinton, then Secretary of State, expressed her support for the Bahraini national dialogue and the efforts of the Crown Prince in that regard.[85] According to Thomas Ambrosio, such statements 'were seemingly designed to reassure Manama that the US-Bahrain relationship was very important to Washington and a continued tendency to exaggerate the significance of positive statements and actions by Bahraini officials.' He argues that the role of the US was instrumental in providing political and diplomatic support as a 'black knight'[86] which helped the Khalifa regime to suppress the protests.

The Saudi military intervention in Bahrain was another nervous moment for the US. Initially, the US was opposed to the military intervention as it feared that it would further aggravate the situation in Bahrain. Secretary of Defence Robert Gates visited Bahrain on March 12, 2011 and met King Hamad and Crown Prince Salman to discuss speeding up political reform in the kingdom. But a few hours after Gates' return home, King Hamad invited the GCC troops to Bahrain. According to Jean-François Seznec, this move was a 'slap on the face' of the US. Highlighting the Saudi disregard for the US, Seznec further contends:

> "The Saudis were called in within a few hours of Gates's departure, however, showing their disdain for his efforts to reach a negotiated solution. By acting so soon after Gates's visit, Saudi Arabia has made the United States look at best irrelevant to events in Bahrain, and from the Shiite opposition's point of view, even complicit in the Saudi military intervention."[87]

The Saudi military intervention was criticised by US policymakers, who did not want a military conflagration in Bahrain. But the authorities in Washington refrained from making any direct comments condemning the GCC military intervention.[88] Some commentators are of the view that the US was informed about the possible Saudi intervention in Bahrain. But the US chose to remain silent for the sake of political stability against democratic reforms in Bahrain for fear of jeopardising its security interests.[89] A few months earlier, Saudi Arabia had urged the US to take action to save Hosni Mubarak in Egypt, but the US did not follow up on this request, and ultimately Mubarak stepped down as President of Egypt. The US silence on the Saudi intervention in Bahrain may have been intended to repair its ties with Saudi Arabia stemming from this development.[90]

Bahrain threw up a diplomatic challenge for the US. As Frederic Wehrey notes, in Bahrain 'the US finds itself in the undesirable position of maintaining close ties with a repressive regime that has skilfully avoided meaningful reforms while engaging in a concerted public relations campaign to burnish its image.'[91] Simon Henderson says that 'the most crucial U.S. challenge is encouraging royal political concessions without jeopardizing the Fifth Fleet headquarters.'[92] The US encourages the resumption of the national dialogue as it is the only formal mechanism of negotiation between the government and the opposition. The US has expressed its concern over the continuing human rights violations in the country. The US has therefore advocated a regime-initiated solution to the crisis.[93] President Barack Obama made his policy clear in his State of the Union Address on February 12, 2013, where he stated that "in the Middle East, we will stand with citizens as they demand their universal rights, and support stable transitions to democracy."[94] Politically sympathising with the demands of the protesters and maintaining a strategic and military partnership with the Khalifa regime is a challenge for the US in Bahrain. Critics point out that the US has maintained silence on the developments in Bahrain and subsequent Saudi military intervention because of its geopolitical interests in Bahrain in particular and the Gulf region in general.[95] The failure of the US to condemn the Saudi-led military intervention and its acceptance of the claims of both Bahraini and Saudi regimes of Iranian intervention in the affairs of Bahrain has disappointed the protesters and opposition in Bahrain.[96] But as the regime of Al Saud and Al Khalifa are allies of the US and the later has several long term political and strategic interests in the Gulf region, the US had only limited options available in its hand at that critical juncture.

Conclusion

Bahrain represents an extremely delicate web of political, social and external factors involved in the continuing sectarian conflict in the kingdom. Even before the outbreak of the protests opposition political groups, on several occasions, have put their demands before the rulers to carry out political and institutional reforms in the country. There have been demands for decades from the majority Shia community to end discrimination against them in various fields. But their demands have not been addressed thereby breeding dissension in their minds against the regime. The crackdown on opposition political figures by the regime, most often on fictitious charges, has made the rulers further unpopular. The government's suspicion of the Shia opposition having established link with their coreligionists in Iran is the main stumbling block for initiating any serious reform. The history of Iranian claim on Bahrain and the failed coup of 1981 by some Shia militants with alleged Iranian backing is still a critical factor in the government's approach towards the majority Shias. Because of few such incidents the government has often questioned the loyalty of the opposition for the country. This has further infuriated the Shias again stirring the never-ending sectarian issue in the country.

It seems like all the elements required for a popular uprising against the regime existed in Bahrain even before the beginning of the protests. The Arab Spring provided a perfect springboard to it. Political environment of Arab mass uprising against the rulers in several countries at the same time was an opportunity for the Bahraini youths, civil society and the political opposition to seize the moment and to put renewed pressure on the regime. The fact that Shia majority population is ruled by a Sunni minority royal family and the majority complains of political and religious discrimination against the regime is a potential situation for sectarian conflict. The involvement of the regional powers further complicates the situation. Regional powers like Saudi Arabia and Iran have significant political and strategic interests in Bahrain. There have been political and diplomatic attempts by both the regional players to sway the situation to their favour. The Saudi support for the regime and Iranian support for the protesters against the regime clearly demarcated the sectarian faultlines in the kingdom. Further, the Saudi military intervention to protect the Khalifa regime and the Iranian condemnation to it brought to the fore the competing interests of both the countries to the fore. The small island kingdom of Bahrain became a theatre of sectarian tussle between two big and powerful neighbours. The regime of King Hamad, receiving political and military support from Saudi Arabia, condemned Iran for its support for the protesters and alleged that it is trying to create instability in the kingdom. Though the protests have ended, the government continues to target the leaders of the opposition. Rather than helping to tranquillise the prevailing unrest, such crackdown has further fuelled the sectarian sentiments in the minds of the people. Holding of the national dialogue amidst crack down on opposition leaders has sounded hollow and window-dressing for the opposition. So the national dialogue could not be completed to reach any consensus. Though the street protests have ended with no immediate threat to the regime, the sectarian tension continues to simmer in the kingdom.

END NOTES

1. "Population and demographics", Ministry of Information Affairs, Kingdom of Bahrain, at http://www.msia.gov.bh/en/Kingdom-of-Bahrain/Pages/Population-and-Demographic-Growth.aspx.
2. Ronald E. Neumann, "Bahrain: A very complicated little island", *Middle East Policy*, 20 (4), Winter 2013, p. 46.
3. Jane Kinninmont, "Bahrain: Rentierism and beyond", in Kjetil Selvik and Bjørn Olav Utvik (eds.), *Oil States in the New Middle East: Uprisings and Stability*, Routledge, New York, 2015, pp. 113-131.
4. Omar Al-Shehabi, "Demography and Bahrain's unrest", Carnegie Endowment for International Peace, March 16, 2011 at http://carnegieendowment.org/sada/?fa=43079.
5. "Almarzooq: Bahrain naturalized 95k foreigners adding 17.3% to population", Al Wefaq, at http://alwefaq.net/cms/2014/08/17/31859/.
6. Michael Herb, "Princes, parliaments, and the prospects for democracy in the Gulf", in Marsha Pripstein Posusney and Michele Penner Angrist (eds.), *Authoritarianism in the Middle East: Regimes and Resistance*, Lynne Reinner, London, 2005, p. 178.
7. Hasan Shafaei, "National Action Charter and Human Rights", Bahrain Human Rights Monitor, at http://www.bahrainmonitor.org/views/w-002-01.html.
8. Magdalena Karolak, "Escalation of social conflict during popular upheavals: Evidence from Bahrain", *CEU Political Science Journal*, 7 (2), 2012, p. 184.
9. "Nine Bahraini Shias stripped of nationality", *Al Jazeera*, September 30, 2014, at http://www.aljazeera.com/news/middleeast/2014/09/nine-bahraini-shias-stripped-nationality-20149304591082478.html.
10. "HM King Hamad declares State of National Safety", *Bahrain News Agency*, March 15, 2011, at http://www.bna.bh/portal/en/news/449960.
11. Mahjoob Zweiri and Mohammed Zahid, "The victory of Al Wefaq: the rise of Shiite politics in Bahrain", Research Institute for European and American Studies, Research Paper No. 108, April 2007, at http://rieas.gr/images/rieas108.pdf.
12. "Bahrain court bans Shiite opposition group", *Middle East Eye*, October 28, 2014, at http://www.middleeasteye.net/news/bahrain-court-bans-shiite-opposition-group-1695462304.
13. "Al-Wefaq: Bahrain crisis is about demands for democracy", at http://alwefaq.net/cmsen/2013/06/12/20679/.
14. "Al Wefaq SG called for a constitutional monarchy and was accused for the opposite", at http://alwefaq.net/cmsen/2015/06/11/44641/.
15. "Ebrahim Sharif re-arrested less than a month after his release", National Democratic Action Society, July 12, 2015, at http://www.aldemokrati.org/en/details.php?artid=7491.
16. "Bahrain's Crown Prince calls for national mourning", *Reuters*, February 19, 2011, at http://www.reuters.com/article/us-bahrain-prince-idUSTRE71I1ZI20110219.
17. "Bahrain King orders release of political prisoners", *Arab News*, February 22, 2011, at http://www.arabnews.com/node/369005.

18. "Three Bahraini ministers sacked in wake of mass protests", *Arabian Business*, February 26, 2011, at http://m.arabianbusiness.com/three-bahraini-ministers-sacked-in-wake-of-mass-protests-383300.html.
19. Report of the Bahrain Independent Commission of Inquiry (BICI), at http://www.bici.org.bh/BICIreportEN.pdf, p.168.
20. "Arrests follow deadly Bahrain crackdown", *Al Jazeera*, March 18, 2011, at http://www.aljazeera.com/news/middleeast/2011/03/201131733318735470.html.
21. "State of emergency declared in Bahrain", *The National*, March 16, 2011, at http://www.thenational.ae/news/world/middle-east/state-of-emergency-declared-in-bahrain.
22. See the Al Wefaq report, "The failed mission: Deleting the opposition", April 1, 2015, at http://alwefaq.net/media/2015/01/Failed_Mission_EN_2015-1.pdf.
23. Laurence Louer, "Sectarianism and coup-proofing strategies in Bahrain", *Journal of Strategic Studies*, 36 (2), 2013, pp. 245-260.
24. Derek Lutterbeck, "Arab uprisings, armed forces, and civil–military relations", *Armed Forces and Society*, 39 (1), 2013, p. 43.
25. Zoltan Barany, "The role of the military", *Journal of Democracy*, 22 (4), October 2011, p. 35.
26. "Tensions high as Bahrain dialogue looms", *Reuters*, July 1, 2011, at http://www.reuters.com/article/us-bahrain-dialogue-idUSTRE76042820110701.
27. "National Dialogue Spokesman: The dialogue aims to reach consensus on a wider range of issues of concern to the Bahraini people", *Bahrain News Agency*, June 30, 2011, at http://www.bna.bh/portal/en/news/463164.
28. Ibid.
29. "Bahrain national dialogue begins", *Al Jazeera*, July 2, 2011, at http://www.aljazeera.com/news/middleeast/2011/07/20117214754858684.html.
30. "Bahrain's main opposition party withdraws from 'national dialogue", *CNN*, July 18, 2011, at http://edition.cnn.com/2011/WORLD/meast/07/18/bahrain.unrest/.
31. Ibid.
32. "The Bahraini regime arrests the Political Assistant of Al-Wefaq's Secretary-General", September 17, 2013, at http://alwefaq.net/cms/2013/09/17/22861/.
33. "The National Democratic Opposition Parties refuse the restriction on political action in Bahrain", September 7, 2013, at http://alwefaq.net/cmsen/2013/09/07/22625/.
34. Ibid.
35. For the full report, see the Bahrain Independent Commission of Inquiry at http://www.bici.org.bh/BICIreportEN.pdf.
36. Ibid.
37. Ibid.
38. Ibid
39. Ibid.
40. "Bahrain opposition societies: Window dressing institutions cannot address crisis", at http://alwefaq.net/cmsen/2016/05/11/45331/.
41. "Bassiouni: Bahrain's progress limited by 'piecemeal' approach to reforms", *Al Monitor*, June 13, 2014, at http://www.al-monitor.com/pulse/originals/2014/06/cherif-bassiouni-bici-bahrain-uprising-violations.html

42. "King Fahd Causeway development plan unveiled", *Bahrain News Agency*, February 10, 2016, at http://www.bna.bh/portal/en/news/710506.
43. Simon Mabon, "The battle for Bahrain: Iranian-Saudi rivalry", *Middle East Policy*, 19 (2), Summer 2012, p. 87.
44. Simon Mabon, *Saudi Arabia and Iran: Power and Rivalry in the Middle East*, I.B. Tauris, London, 2016, p. 71.
45. Graham E. Fuller and Rend Rahim Francke, *The Arab Shia: The Forgotten Muslims*, Macmillan, London, 1999, p. 180.
46. Madawi Al-Rasheed and Loulouwa Al-Rasheed, "The politics of encapsulation: Saudi policy towards tribal and religious opposition", *Middle Eastern Studies*, 32 (1), January 1996, p. 111.
47. Neil Quilliam and Maggie Kamel, "Modernising legitimacy: Saudi strategies", *Alternatives: Turkish Journal of International Relations*, 2 (2), Summer 2003, at www.alternativesjournal.net/volume2/number2/kamel.htm.
48. Madawi Al Rasheed, "The Shia of Saudi Arabia: A minority in search of cultural authenticity", *British Journal of Middle Eastern Studies*, 25 (1), 1998, p. 134; Simon Mabon, "Kingdom in crisis? The Arab Spring and instability in Saudi Arabia", *Contemporary Security Policy*, 33 (3), 2012, p. 541.
49. Marina Ottaway, "Bahrain: Between the United States and Saudi Arabia", Carnegie Endowment for International Peace, April 4, 2011, at http://carnegieendowment.org/2011/04/04/bahrain-between-united-states-and-saudi-arabia#.
50. "Popular protests in North Africa and the Middle East (III): The Bahrain Revolt", International Crisis Group, Middle East/North Africa Report No 105, April 6, 2011, at http://www.crisisgroup.org/~/media/Files/105-%20Popular%20 Protests%20 in%20North%20Africa%20and%20the%20Middle%20East%20-III-The%20Bahrain%20Revolt.ashx.
51. Mohammed Nuruzzaman, "Politics, economics and Saudi military intervention in Bahrain", *Journal of Contemporary Asia*, 43 (2), 2013, p.6.
52. Rachel Bronson, "Saudi Arabia's intervention in Bahrain: A necessary evil or a strategic blunder?" Foreign Policy Research Institute, March 2011, at http://old.fpri.org/articles/2011/03/saudi-arabias-intervention-bahrain-necessary-evil-or-strategic-blunder-0#.
53. Turki Al Faisal bin Abdul Aziz Al Saud, "Saudi Arabia's Foreign Policy", *Middle East Policy*, 64 (4), Winter 2013, p. 42.
54. Brandon Friedman, "Battle for Bahrain: What one uprising meant for the Gulf States and Iran", *World Affairs*, 174 (6), March-April 2012, pp. 74-84.
55. "GCC Foreign Ministers reject foreign interference and appropriate $20 billion for development in Bahrain and Oman", *Saudi Press Agency*, March 10, 2011, at http://www.spa.gov.sa/viewstory.php?newsid=872396.
56. Friedman, n. 54, p. 77.
57. See the full GCC statement at https://www.gcc-sg.org/eng/index15af.html.
58. Brandon Friedman, n. 50, pp. 74-84.
59. "GCC pledges $20 billion in aid for Oman, Bahrain", *Gulf News*, March 10, 2011, at http://gulfnews.com/news/gulf/saudi-arabia/gcc-pledges-20billion-in-aid-for-oman-bahrain-1.774648.
60. GCC Secretary General hails National Dialogue", *Bahrain News Agency*, July 1, 2011, at https://www.bna.bh/portal/en/news/463250.

61. Ibid.
62. Statement by Ayatollah Khamenei, "Islamic awareness will thwart enemies' plots", The Office of the Supreme Leader, Grand Ayatollah Sayyid Ali Hosseini Khamenei, April 23, 2011, at http://www.leader.ir/en/content/7993/Islamic-awareness-will-thwart-enemies'-plots.
63. Ibid.
64. Shahram Chubin and Charles Tripp, *Iran-Saudi Arabia Relations and Regional Order*, Routledge, New York, 2014, p. 34.
65. "Iran lawmakers support Bahrain protests", *PressTV*, at http://edition.presstv.ir/detail.fa/170743.html.
66. "Iran seeks immediate OIC, APA meeting on Bahrain", *Iranian Students' News Agency*, March 19, 2011, at http://isna.ir/en/news/8912-17882/Iran-seeks-im2mediate-OIC-APA-meeting-on.
67. "ME simmering with anti-Saudi sentiments", *PressTV*, March 17, 2011, at http://edition.presstv.com/detail/170424.html.
68. "Interior Minister: Iran's interference in Bahrain supported by strong evidence", *Bahrain News Agency*, February 21, 2016, at http://www.bna.bh/portal/en/news/712215.
69. Ibid.
70. See the full report of the BICI at http://www.bici.org.bh/BICIreportEN.pdf.
71. Jane Kinninmont, "Bahrain: Beyond the impasse", The Royal Institute of International Affairs, June 2012, at https://www.chathamhouse.org/sites/files/chathamhouse/public/Research/Middle%20East/pr0612kinninmont.pdf.
72. Hasan Tariq Alhasan, "The role of Iran in the failed coup of 1981: The IFLB in Bahrain", *Middle East Journal*, 65 (4), 2011, p. 603.
73. Laurence Louer, "The State and sectarian identities in the Persian Gulf monarchies: Bahrain, Saudi Arabia and Kuwait in comparative perspective", in Lawrence G. Potter (ed.) *Sectarian Politics in the Persian Gulf*, Oxford University Press, New York, 2014, p. 125.
74. Michael Rubin, "Are Bahraini Shi'ites puppets of Iran?", American Enterprise Institute for Public Policy Research, June 2014, at https://www.aei.org/wp-content/uploads/2014/06/-are-bahraini-shiites-puppets-of-iran_100707902786.pdf.
75. Majid Khadduri, "Iran's claim to the sovereignty of Bahrayn", *American Journal of International Law*, 45 (4), 1951, pp. 631-647.
76. Edward Gordon, "Resolution of the Bahrain dispute", *American Journal of International Law*, 65 (3), 1971, pp. 560-568.
77. Faisal bin Salman al-Saud, *Iran, Saudi Arabia and the Gulf: Power Politics in Transition*, I.B. Tauris, London, 2004, p. 54.
78. Mabon, n. 43, p. 88.
79. "U.S. relations with Bahrain", Bureau of Near Eastern Affairs, US Department of State, July 31, 2015, at http://www.state.gov/r/pa/ei/bgn/26414.htm.
80. Alexander Cooley and Daniel H. Nexon, "Bahrain's base politics: The Arab Spring and America's military bases", *Foreign Affairs*, April 5, 2015, at https://www.foreignaffairs.com/articles/djibouti/2011-04-05/bahrains-base-politics.
81. "U.S. relations with Bahrain", n. 79.
82. Kenneth Katzman, "Bahrain: Reform, security, and U.S. policy", Congressional

Research Service, March 18, 2016, at https://www.fas.org/sgp/crs/mideast/95-1013.pdf.

83. "Lifting holds on security assistance to the Government of Bahrain", Press Statement by John Kirby, US Department of State, Washington D.C., June 29, 2015, at http://www.state.gov/r/pa/prs/ps/2015/06/244478.htm.
84. See the press statement by Philip J. Crowley, Assistant Secretary of State for Public Affairs, US Department of State, February 15, 2011, at http://www.state.gov/r/pa/prs/ps/2011/02/156626.htm.
85. See the statement by Secretary of State Hillary Clinton with Crown Prince Salman, June 7, 2011, at http://www.state.gov/secretary/20092013clinton/rm/2011/06/165215.htm.
86. Thomas Ambrosio, "Democratic states and authoritarian firewalls: America as a black knight in the uprising in Bahrain", *Contemporary Politics*, 20(3), 2014, pp. 331-346.
87. Jean-François Seznec, "Saudi Arabia strikes back", *Foreign Policy*, March 14, 2011, at http://foreignpolicy.com/2011/03/14/saudi-arabia-strikes-back-2/.
88. "U.S.-Saudi tensions intensify with Mideast turmoil", *New York Times*, March 4, 2011, at http://www.nytimes.com/2011/03/15/world/middleeast/15saudi.html.
89. Cooley and Nexon, n. 80.
90. "Why US silence on Bahrain's crackdown could backfire", *Christian Science Monitor*, April 14, 2011, at http://www.csmonitor.com/World/Middle-East/2011/0414/Why-US-silence-on-Bahrain-s-crackdown-could-backfire.
91. Frederic Wehrey, "The precarious ally: Bahrain's impasse and U.S. policy", Carnegie Endowment for International Peace, February 6, 2013, at http://carnegieendowment.org/2013/02/06/precarious-ally-bahrain-s-impasse-and-u.s.-policy#.
92. Simon Henderson, "Bahrain's royal politics and the U.S. Navy Base", *The Washington Institute for Near East Policy, Policy Watch 2045*, March 12, 2013, at http://www.washingtoninstitute.org/policy-analysis/view/bahrains-royal-politics-and-the-u.s.-navy-base.
93. "U.S. Policy toward the Arabian Peninsula: Yemen and Bahrain", Hearing before the Subcommittee on the Middle East and North Africa, of the Committee on Foreign Affairs, House of Representatives, November 19, 2013, at http://docs.house.gov/meetings/FA/FA13/20131119/101521/HHRG-113-FA13-Transcript-20131119.pdf.
94. "Remarks by the President in the State of the Union Address", The White House, February 12, 2103, at https://www.whitehouse.gov/the-press-office/2013/02/12/remarks-president-state-union-address.
95. Jeffrey Bachman and Matar Ebrahim Matar, "The US must not bear silent witness to another crackdown in Bahrain", *The Guardian*, August 12, 2013, at http://www.theguardian.com/commentisfree/2013/aug/12/bahrain-silent-witness-crackdown-bahrain.
96. Stephen Zunes, "Bahrain's Arrested Revolution", *Arab Studies Quarterly*, 35 (2), Spring 2013, p. 158.

3

Yemen: Political Instability and Sectarian Strife

Since the unification of the country in 1990, politics in Yemen has been shaped by a combination of an authoritarian political system, tribal identities of the local people, and competing regional and extra-regional powers. Being the poorest country in the Arabian Peninsula among its oil-rich Gulf neighbours, Yemen has been susceptible to the contesting interests of the regional big powers. During the Cold War, there was interference in its affairs by the regional powers such as Saudi Arabia and Egypt and world powers like Britain, the United States and the Soviet Union. Historically, the present-day Yemen was two countries, known as Yemen Arab Republic (YAR) or North Yemen and People's Democratic Republic of Yemen (PDRY) or South Yemen. The northern part was under the Ottomans till 1918. After the collapse of the Ottoman Empire, Imam Yahya, leader of the Zaydi community, took over power there. Yahya was assassinated in 1948. His son Imam Ahmed succeeded him and ruled till his death in 1962. In the same year, the Imamate system was overthrown in coup by Army officers who then captured power and declared the country a republic, to be known officially as Yemen Arab Republic. The southern part of present-day Yemen was under the control of the British, who decided to withdraw in 1967. After the British withdrew from south Yemen, the Communists captured power and changed the name of the country to

People's Democratic Republic of Yemen on December 1, 1970. YAR and PDRY remained hostile to each other and in 1972 fought a war. The Arab League brokered a ceasefire between the two countries, and after years of hostility, the two sides agreed to unify as a single country. Yemen was declared a republic on May 22, 1990 and Ali Abdullah Saleh of the YAR became its first President.

Traditionally, Yemen has been a tribal society where tribal loyalties and allegiances play a crucial role in the social and political life of the country.[1] Relationship among tribes and their leaders are crucial factors in Yemeni local and national politics. These traditional ties outweigh their political affiliations and tribal loyalties retain a predominant place in politics, society and in Yemeni collective mind.[2] Historically, sect-based identity has not played a prominent role in the politics of Yemen. Though there were a number of political parties formed on religious and sectarian lines, the sectarian politics in Yemen was confined to the closed political circles only.[3] The Houthis, who belong to the Zaidi Shia sect, started a political and religious movement in the early 1990s in the Saada province. They were also armed and became involved in violent activities often targeting the security forces. Such activities on the part of the Houthis gave rise to the sectarian tensions in the country. The situation began to aggravate after the outbreak of the protests in the country in 2011. The sectarian divisions began to become more pronounced as people from different sects began to identify themselves on the basis of their sectarian affiliations and some hardliner groups started to draw people towards them to fight against the other groups.[4] This led to the conception of a strong sectarian identity among the people in the country.

Even after being unified as a single republic, Yemen remained an authoritarian political system under Saleh who wielded massive power. There were severe allegations of corruption against Saleh. The economy did not show any signs of significant growth and it mainly depended on the revenue generated from oil. There was an increase in unemployment rate and frustration was running high among the youths. At the same time, there was a growing dissension among the people of the south who alleged political and economic discrimination against them. Taking the opportunity of a state that is economically and militarily weak, Al-Qaeda spread its network in the country. The regime received huge amounts of aid from the US and Saudi Arabia to fight terrorism and extremism in the country. But Saleh remained unsuccessful in containing their activities and Yemen remained a safe haven for Al-Qaeda. The Houthis protested against Saleh's close relationship with the US and Saudi Arabia. They also complained of political and economic marginalisation by the government and started an armed movement against the government. Thus, even after the unification of the country, Saleh continuously faced political and security challenges.

Beginning of the Protests

Protests against President Saleh began in January 2011 after the fall of the regimes of Zine Ben Ali of Tunisia and Hosni Mubarak of Egypt. Inspired by the success of the protests in these two countries, thousands of protesters came on the streets calling for political and economic reforms in the country and demanding Saleh's resignation. Most of the protesters were educated youth who were frustrated with Saleh's autocratic rule, corruption, economic underdevelopment, and unemployment in the country. Within days, the protests drew more support from the people and they quickly spread throughout the country. A nervous Saleh pledged political and constitutional reforms in the country. He also promised not to stand for presidency when his term would expire in 2013 and that his son Ahmad would not succeed him in office. He also called upon the protesters to come to the negotiating table. But none of his assurances was convincing to the protesters who demanded nothing but his resignation.

As the protests aggravated, Saleh used his security forces to control the protesters. Security forces and the protesters clashed on Sanaa's streets violently for weeks resulting in many deaths. There were a number of clashes between the protesters and Saleh's supporters, which stimulated further violent protests against the regime. The coercive tactics employed by the Saleh regime eroded his legitimacy among the masses and he was seen as losing his grip on power. On March 20, 2012 Major General Ali Mohsen Al Ahmar, one of the most powerful military Generals of Saleh and the commander of the Army's

First Armoured Division, defected and announced his support for the opposition, which would include providing security to the protesters. Following his defection, on the same day, several other senior army officers followed suit. These included General Ali Abdullaha Aliewa, adviser to the army chief, Brig. Hameed Al Koshebi (Brigade 310 in Omran area), Brig. Mohammed Ali Mohsen (Eastern Division) and Brig. Nasser Eljahori (Brigade 121).[5] The defections of such high ranking officers had critical effect on the rank-and-file of the military. With such loss of morale in the army, the government quickly lost access to most of the units in the north-western and eastern regions of the country.[6] After a lot of political and diplomatic efforts by Saudi Arabia and the Gulf Cooperation Council (GCC), Saleh finally agreed to step down as President and hand over power to the Vice-President. In November 2012, he stepped down and signed the "GCC Initiative" to pave the way for democratic transition in the country.

As the protests gathered momentum, sectarian divisions became more pronounced, as people from different sects began to identify themselves on sectarian lines and some hardliner groups started to draw people to fight against the other groups.[7] The advance of the Houthis from their stronghold Saada in north Yemen to capital Sanaa in late 2014 has been the last nail in the coffin of Yemeni stability.

GCC Initiative and the National Dialogue Conference

President Saleh stepped down from office in February 2012 after the GCC intervened and signed a deal with Saleh. The removal of President Ali Abdullah Saleh in 2012 following the pact did not meet the aspirations of the people. The logjam was broken with the proposal of the GCC which was supported by all major powers. The deal, came to be known as the 'GCC Initiative', included the details of Yemen's transition process. Saleh agreed to step down as the president and hand over power to Vice-President Abdo Mansour Hadi. The signing of the GCC Initiative also drew criticism, since many believed that Saudi Arabia was 'trying to influence the outcome of political change' in Yemen.[8] In January 2012, Parliament approved the controversial law which gave Saleh complete immunity from prosecution in return for stepping down[9] and paving the way for the transition process. The law also provides political immunity to his aides in the civil services or military, though they can be charged for committing any criminal or terrorist acts.[10] Human Rights Watch described the law as 'licence to kill'.[11] Amnesty International stated that the immunity is a 'bitter blow for those calling for justice for human rights violations over recent years.'[12] In the view of some other commentators, the immunity was 'a dialogue between elites; elites in Sana'a and elites in the Gulf states'.[13] In Charles Schmitz's view, the GCC Initiative was:

> "an agreement between the competing elite factions of the old Saleh regime that had split into warring sides during the Arab Spring...In the end, the divided Yemeni elite and their foreign supporters, particularly the United States and Saudi Arabia, negotiated the Gulf initiative, not the leaders of the street protests. As a result, the impetus of the initiative was to guarantee the interests of the Yemeni elite and the United States and Saudi Arabia, not implement the changes demanded by the protestors."[14]

The GCC Initiative called for a phased transition and transfer of power. It gave Vice-President Hadi all the powers and authority of the President and urged that the transition would be complete in two phases. In the first phase, a national unity government was to be formed and it would take decisions by consensus. Its responsibilities were to ensure cessation of violence, facilitate humanitarian access, and issue appropriate legal and administrative instructions, among others. The Vice-President was to have all powers relating to foreign affairs, economic affairs and military affairs and would be responsible for holding the National Dialogue Conference (NDC). The NDC would discuss issues of drafting the constitution, constitutional reform, Southern Movement, Houthis, democratic reforms, national reconciliation and protection of rights of the vulnerable groups and sustainable economic development.[15] The presidential elections were to be held within 90 days of the signature of the GCC Initiative. In the second phase, the newly elected president shall exercise all the customary functions as per the constitution. The document laid particular focus on holding a national dialogue conference to discuss issues of drafting the constitution, constitutional reform, southern movement, Houthis, democratic reforms, national reconciliation and protection of rights of the vulnerable groups and sustainable economic development.

The NDC was held from March 18, 2013 to January 24, 2014, involving all the major political parties, groups and other stakeholders to build consensus over the future roadmap for the country. As agreed in the power transfer deal mediated by the GCC, the NDC included all the political parties, civil society representatives, southern movement, Houthis, women and youths. A total of 565 delegates, representing different sections of society, were involved in the dialogue. The NDC discussed nine issues, as follows: (i) the Southern issue, (ii) the Saada (Houthi) issue, (iii) transitional justice, (iv) state building, (v) good governance, (vi) military and security, (vii) independence of special entities (focusing on the rights of vulnerable groups, including children, minorities and displaced persons), (viii) rights and freedoms, and (ix) development.[16]

The NDC was expected to come out with a final document in six months of time, but it failed to meet the deadline because of repeated disruptions and walkouts especially by the Houthis and the Southerners. In January 2014, the NDC's final document was accepted by the plenary. It was indeed a stupendous accomplishment. President Hadi described it as the 'beginning of the road to build a new Yemen'.[17]

The NDC's outcome document was handed over to a Constitution Drafting Committee (CDC) for follow-up. As per the GCC Initiative, the draft constitution should have been discussed and placed for referendum. But the Houthis were not in agreement with the crucial issues of the country's federal structure. A committee headed by President Hadi proposed Yemen to be divided into six zones, as follows: four northern – Azal, Saba, Janad and Tahama – and two southern – Aden and Hadramawt. Both the Houthis and the Southerners rejected it. Houthi leader Mohammed Al Bakheiti said that the plan 'divides Yemen into poor and wealthy' regions. The Southerners said that the proposal did not meet their aspirations.[18]

The Houthis captured the capital city Sanaa in September 2014. This instantly escalated violence throughout the country and nullified the NDC's achievements. In January 2015, the Houthis took over the presidential palace in Sanaa. On February 6, 2015, they declared dissolution of Parliament. They also declared that a five-member Presidential Council would replace President Hadi for an interim period of two years and a 'revolutionary committee' would be in charge of forming a new parliament.[19] Hadi was placed under house arrest but was later released, and then fled to Aden. This pushed the country into further political instability and increasing violence. The transition process received a severe jolt with the Houthi takeover of the capital.

Houthis and their Advance to Sanaa

The Houthis belong to the Zaidi Shia sect.[20] They are fighting against the government, accusing it of widespread corruption, socio-economic negligence of the Shias, permitting the growing influence of Sunni Wahhabism in the country and allying with the USA. In the 1990s, they started their movement in Saada province in response to the growing Salafi influence in the region. The Houthis hold that the only legitimate Islamic rule is rule by an Imam.[21] In 2004, Hussein Badreddin Al Houthi launched an armed uprising against the Saleh regime. The security situation in Yemen worsened since then with frequent clashes between the Houthis and the government's forces. Attempts by the government to maintain stability by reaching a ceasefire agreement with the Houthi rebels have failed miserably.

The Houthis have been accused by the government of intending to create a separate state in northern Yemen. The government sees them as having links with Iran.[22] The erstwhile Saleh regime clashed with the Houthis on a number of occasions, trying to neutralise them politically and militarily. In 2010 the Houthis signed a six-point agreement with the government but that agreement fell apart. The popular uprising in 2011 created an opportunity for the Houthis as they joined the protests against Saleh. They have capitalised upon the existing political chaos and power vacuum in the country and have worked 'to broaden their popular appeal, defined a political programme and claimed their place in the national mainstream.'[23] The Houthis exploited the unstable situation which was witnessed in Yemen. Yemeni economy was faltering and Saleh was found heavily dependent on foreign aid which was mainly provided by Saudi Arabia and the US. There was high unemployment in the country with poor socio-economic conditions. The country had become a safe haven for Al-Qaeda, with Al-Qaeda in the Arabian Peninsula (AQAP) operating from Yemen not facing strong military action from the state. In the south, the Southern Movement was gaining ground who demanded autonomy. The Southern Movement occasionally became violent, which emerged as another challenge for the government. Because of such prolonged economic, social and security challenges faced by the country, Yemen became a failed state. The authorities failed to inject any stability into the marauding socio-economic problems as well as the internal security challenges emerging from Al-Qaeda, Southern Movement and the Houthis. Such a situation of internal social, economic and security challenges was not easy for Saleh to handle and the situation was exploited by the Houthis.

Another objective of the Houthis' is their fight against the Salafis, who are followers of a strict interpretation of Sunni Islam. Dammaj City was the centre of a violent conflict between the two groups, which began in 2011. Dammaj lies close to Saada province, a Houthi stronghold. The Houthis allege that the Salafis have brought a large number of foreign fighters to Dammaj to fight against them. The Salafis claim that the foreigners are people who come to study at the Dar Al Hadith seminary.[24] The Houthi attack on Dammaj with heavy weapons and blockaded the city and led to aggravation of the conflict resulting in killing of hundreds of people from both the sides. In January 2014, the government mediated a ceasefire and also deployed troops to monitor it.[25] Heavy fighting has also taken place in Taiz City in the east of the country, where the Salafis are fighting alongside the government forces.

The capability of the Houthis to launch an armed campaign was a cause of concern for the government, who feared that this may derail the efforts towards peace. Though the Houthis joined the NDC, they refused to disarm. After several failed negotiations, President Hadi, Prime Minister Khaled Bahah and the cabinet resigned in January 2015. After the Houthi capture of the capital, President Hadi fled to Aden, and with the situation worsening day by day, he moved to Riyadh, requesting the GCC to intervene in Yemen. Saudi Arabia then decided to intervene militarily to push the Houthis out of Sanaa.

The Houthis' military success from Saada to Sanaa was made easier because of the collaboration of former president Saleh and his son Ahmad Ali Saleh, who is the former commander of the Republican Guard. There are still some sections of the Yemeni military who are loyal to the Saleh family. Three of Saleh's nephews also commanded other elite military units. Even after being removed from power, Saleh still retained a lot of influence among some sections of the military. As a result of the immunity he received, Saleh also continued to head the General People's Congress (GPC). The GPC controls a 'strong patronage network and maintains extensive ties throughout the bureaucracy, religious circles and among the tribal leaders.'[26] Saleh's primary strength had been his control over the 'best equipped and efficient elements from military and security services.'[27] He has used his influence over the sections of military and provided support to the Houthis' advance to the capital.[28] Heading the GPC enabled him to manipulate his military and tribal allies to preserve his power in the country. Saleh is doing everything possible to undermine and thwart the process of transition, thereby making his point that no change or transition would be possible in the country without his support. Saleh continues with his divide-and-rule approach in Yemen. Earlier, he used to support the Islah party, founded by Abdullah Ibn Husain Al Ahmar and Ali Mohsen Al Ahmar, against the Houthis. And now he is supporting the Houthis against the Islah party.[29]

Saudi Concerns in an Unstable Yemen

For Saudi Arabia, an unstable Yemen remains a source of threat to its national security. Therefore, Saudi Arabia has a history of intervening in the Yemeni internal affairs even before the unification of the North and South Yemen in to the modern Yemen by cultivating a 'vast network of patronage with tens of influential Sheikhly families.'[30] This tribal patronage network has helped Saudi Arabia to keep a tab on the internal political dynamics of Yemen. Traditionally, Saudi policy towards Yemen has been driven by its desire to maintain stability in the weak state rather than using it as a regional theatre of conflict. It has heavily invested with the regime and political elites in Yemen in exchange for political influence. Riyadh has devoted a lot of money and political capital to spread Salafi and Wahhabi network in Yemen.[31]

The friendship between Saleh regime and Riyadh served the interests of both. While Saudi Arabia was able manage its Yemen policies to avoid any threat emanating from its southern neighbour, Saleh received huge amounts of economic aid and political support from Riyadh.

Immediately after the beginning of the protests against the Saleh regime, Saudi Arabia did meticulously realise the potential challenge emanating from Yemen. Since then the situation in Yemen has only deteriorated and the Saudi concerns have grown proportionately. Riyadh played a central role in the success of the GCC Initiative. At present, Riyadh wants to restore the legitimacy of the Hadi government for stability in the country. Though historically Riyadh has wanted to keep Yemen internally weak and financially dependent on it, with the situation going out of hand this time, it wants Yemen to remain relatively stable and a dependent ally of the kingdom. Thus, Riyadh believes it is important that the Hadi regime to be restored as the legitimate government of Yemen and the political process of determining the future roadmap for the country can continue simultaneously. In the present situation of increasing violence and political instability, Riyadh would want a friendly regime in Sanaa which will remain financially dependent upon the kingdom.[32] But as the Houthis captured Sanaa, and the violence continues unabated throughout the country, restoring normalcy would be the top priority for Riyadh.

The advance of the Houthis towards capital Sanaa was taken as a serious challenge by Saudi Arabia. Riyadh perceives the Houthis as an Iranian proxy in Yemen operating with active political, financial and ideological support from Tehran. Therefore, Houthi capture of territories and heavy weapons poses a security threat for the kingdom. Further fragmentation of Yemen in political and sectarian lines will expose the country to possible interference by outside players, particularly, Iran. By deciding to counter the Houthi challenge, Saudi Arabia also took steps to neutralise Iranian influence in its southern neighbourhood. The main concern of Riyadh is that Tehran may exploit the situation to its strategic advantage and cause trouble for the Kingdom. Furthermore, Saudi Arabia is also concerned that an unstable Yemen may be used by criminals, refugees, smugglers, pirates, etc.[33]

Thus, a sectarian political angle is also visible in the conflict in Yemen today with the involvement of Iran and Saudi Arabia. Though both the countries discard the manifestation of any sectarian dimension of the conflict, Yemen seems to be yet another theatre of sectarian conflict between Iran and Saudi Arabia. Besides, Riyadh's militarily intervention was also driven by the growing activities of Al-Qaeda which capitalised upon the existing political uncertainty and violence. Al-Qaeda's open threat to target the House of Saud has remained persisting challenge for the Saudi royal family to ignore.

Saudi Arabia and Houthis

Saudi Arabia has a longstanding hostility with the Houthis. It has fought the Saada war against the Houthis in November 2009 after the Houthis killed a Saudi border guard, following which Saudi Arabia responded with a heavy airstrike on them in north Yemen. The fighting continued till January 2010, when the Houthis offered truce. Despite the truce, the Saudi perception towards the Houthis has not changed at all. Saudi Arabia still believes that the Houthis are proxies of Iran and are a challenge to Yemeni stability and Saudi national security. The capture of large parts of Sanaa and forcing President Hadi to flee the capital was the redline for Saudi Arabia to accept. Saudi Arabia, upon Hadi's request, militarily intervened in Yemen under Operation Decisive Storm with the objective to push the Houthis from Sanaa and destroy the heavy weapons captured by them. Saudi military involvement still continues in Yemen though with limited success. But the Saudi military intervention has a long term repercussion for Yemen's security and its future political roadmap. The Saudi political and military involvement in Yemen has drawn sharp criticism from Iran who supports the inclusion of the Houthis in all the future political processes. These developments have sharply divided the Yemeni politics and society with sectarian conflict taking strong roots in the country. This new phenomenon of sectarian conflict is severely damaging the political process and social fabric of Yemen.

Saudi-led Military Coalition

Initially, Saudi intervention in Yemen was confined to political counsel and economic aid. But with the Houthi advance to the capital it got escalated to a military intervention. A formal request from President Hadi to his neighbours made it easier for Saudi Arabia to invite other Arab countries and to form a coalition to fight against the Houthis in Yemen. The main intention of the Saudis was to push the Houthis back to Saada, their traditional stronghold. The presence of the Houthis in the Yemeni capital was neither politically nor militarily acceptable to the Saudis. The Saudi-led coalition included UAE, Bahrain, Kuwait, Qatar, Egypt, Jordan, Morocco, Senegal and Sudan. Saudi Arabia invited Pakistan to join, but the Pakistan parliament barred the move. Pakistan is an old ally of Saudi Arabia, with strong military ties between the two countries. There are some reasons behind the Pakistani refusal to join the operation in Yemen. Though Pakistan has been a trusted ally of Saudi Arabia, it lately has been trying to engage with Iran for several reasons. Pakistan is trying to balance its engagements with Saudi Arabia and Iran as it has substantial long term interests with both the countries. The Iran-Pakistan gas pipeline (also known as the 'Peace Pipeline') is of major interest to Pakistan. Pakistan and Iran also look forward to their cooperation in Afghanistan. Further, given the sectarian tensions prevailing in Pakistan itself, participating in an operation alongside Saudi Arabia would have sent a different signal to its own domestic population as well. While declining the Saudi request for military support, the Pakistani parliament offered to mediate in the Yemeni conflict and help in the dialogue process. This was not, however, what Riyadh expected from Pakistan at the crucial juncture. Pakistani participation would have certainly strengthened the Saudi position but its refusal came as a shock for Riyadh. In the aftermath of the Pakistani decision, Prime Minister Nawaz Sharif visited Riyadh on April 23, 2015 along with his Defence Minister and Army Chief as a conciliatory move. By undertaking the visit, Pakistan wanted to reassure its commitment towards Saudi security as well as towards its relationship with Riyadh.

Oman also decided not to join the Saudi-led coalition against the Houthis. Oman believes that the conflict in Yemen should be resolved through negotiations and dialogue between the parties concerned. Omani Foreign Minister Yusuf bin Alawi stated that peace efforts and a military campaign 'do not meet' and that 'Oman is a nation of peace'.[34] Most Omanis follow the Ibadi[35] sect of Islam and do not want to be drawn into a regional conflict on sectarian lines between Shias and Sunnis. Like its neighbours Qatar and Saudi Arabia, Oman is also trying its hand in mediating regional conflicts. It has been successful in bringing Iran and the US to the negotiating table over the Iranian nuclear issue. This has led to a creation of the Omani national image as a peaceful and neutral player in the region. To support the Saudi-led military operation would have questioned its credentials as a neutral player. In a region that is fragile and conflict prone, Oman intends to maintain a peaceful and non-interventionist foreign policy. Further, it will be at the receiving end if the conflict further escalates and refugees start flooding into Oman.[36] Till now Oman maintains its neutrality and has rejected the Saudi request to join the military campaign against the Houthis.

Operation Decisive Storm

Operation Decisive Storm started on March 26, 2015. The operation was intended to stop the Houthis capture more territories and flush them out of the capital. As the Houthis captured a large number of heavy weapons such as ballistic missiles from the Yemeni Army, it was a concern that they might use them against their compatriots. Another major objective of the coalition was to destroy the heavy weapons captured by the Houthis. The operation also intended to act against the terrorist organisations and to resume a political process in the country in accordance with the GCC Initiative and the results of the NDC.

The Operation Decisive Storm could only achieve limited success, though Saudi Arabia declared that all of the Houthis' heavy weapons had been destroyed. It continued for 27 days before it was ended. Saudi Arabia probably expected to flush out the Houthis from Sanaa rather easily but the Houthis have proved to be more stubborn and resilient than Riyadh initially believed. Houthis put up a strong challenge more robust than Riyadh would have initially calculated. The Houthis have shown significant endurance capability in the face of attacks by the coalition forces. During the operation, the coalition forces imposed a naval blockade, restrictions on Yemen's airspace and conducted aerial strikes. Riyadh also mobilised support from the neighbouring GCC countries such as Bahrain, Kuwait, Qatar and UAE. Other Arab countries Egypt, Jordan, Senegal, Sudan and Somalia also joined the coalition. US agreed to provide intelligence support to the coalition. Iran along with Russia and China opposed the Saudi-led coalition strikes in Yemen. But the Houthis showed significant endurance. They continued their march to capture and control more territories and captured Aden in April 2015.

The military intervention by the Saudi-led coalition marks an important departure for the present day Yemen. It not only affected the political and security situation of Yemen but also affected the regional geopolitics in West Asia. Restoring the legitimacy of the Hadi regime may be a first step towards bringing back the internal order in Yemen, but the real challenge lies in bringing back all the stakeholders to the table and reach a consensus on future roadmap. The coalition's excessive focus on the military approach may prove detrimental in this regard. The huge political and economic clout of the coalition members in the region show the potential of the coalition to influence large sections of Yemeni society. There is a need for a tactical shift of the coalition's focus from military centric to a political and diplomatic approach in Yemen.

Operation Restoring Hope

After ending the Operation Desert Storm, the coalition announced Operation Restoring Hope. Though the coalition officially declared the end of Operation Decisive Storm on April 21, 2015, the military strikes continued against the Houthis. The new operation intended to protect the citizens, continue to combat terrorism and to engage in a political negotiation to restore peace and stability in the country. It also intended to facilitate evacuation of foreigners and provide humanitarian assistance.[37] The coalition also announced that the operation would seek international cooperation to prevent any weapons delivered to Houthis via air or sea route.

Thus, Operation Restoring Hope is wider in scope covering a larger spectrum of issues covering both military and non-military initiatives by the coalition while Operation Decisive Storm focused primarily on the military aspect of countering Houthi advance. The widened scope of the operation brings more acceptability for the coalition by the Yemenis. But, at the same time, the military offensive by the coalition continues against the Houthis. Many people have been killed because of the coalition air strikes, which has further aggravated the humanitarian crisis in Yemen.

Iran and the Yemen conflict

Iran's religious connection with the Houthis is historical. The Houthis generally have been inspired by Iran's Islamic Revolution and are anti-Western and anti-Saudi. Many Zaidi Shia clerics have received their religious training in Qom in Iran. This is an important channel of continuing Iranian influence among the Houthis in Yemen.[38] A Houthi leader, Abu Sulaiman, disclosed that the Houthis get support from Iran, which also included medium and heavy weapons, and that elements from Iranian-backed Hezbollah and Al Quds provided them expertise to manufacture weapons and train them militarily. He also stated that there was an Iranian plan to create a Shiite state between Saudi Arabia and Yemen in Sada province, including large areas of Al Jawf, Marib, and Hajja and the Saudi provinces of Najran and Jazaan.[39] In November 2009, Hamoud Al Hitar, Yemen's Minister of Religious Affairs, stated that "the Houthis have an expansionist agenda and this was evident when they started fighting Saudi Arabia; it shows that they want to create a state in northern Yemen and southern Saudi Arabia."[40] Despite the allegations, neither Iran nor the Houthis have acknowledged their political, ideological or military linkages. Yemeni and Saudi leaders strongly believe that without Iranian support, Houthis cannot survive such a long drawn military campaign against the coalition.

Supporting the Houthis in Saudi Arabia's backyard would give Iran a geostrategic advantage vis-à-vis Saudi Arabia. Iran has warned all regional countries not to interfere in Yemen. Iranian Foreign Minister Manoucher Mottaki stated that regional countries should not interfere in Yemen's internal affairs as instability in any country in the region will affect security of the entire region. At the same time Iran has suggested that Yemen should 'rehabilitate relations' with its public, including its Shia minority. Yemen, on its part, has clarified that the confrontation with the Houthis is not a sectarian war rather it is a law-enforcement operation against the Houthis who are undermining the security and stability of the country.[41]

The intervention by Saudi Arabia in Yemen has led to a lot of geopolitical tremors in the region. Saudi Arabia has managed to bring many countries to its side who have also contributed to Operation Decisive Storm. On the Other hand, Iran has condemned the Saudi-led military intervention in Yemen. Iranian leaders called for peace and stability in Yemen and at the same time their support for the Houthis strengthened. Further deterioration of the situation in Yemen opened it for a potential sectarian war in the country. The already strained Saudi-Iran relationship got further stressed because of their support for the opposite groups in Yemen.

As both have divergent interests over the situation in Yemen, the Saudi-Iran tension again increased with the Saudi military intervention against the Houthis. While Saudi Arabia supports the status quo in Yemen by supporting the Hadi government, Iran on its part has backed the Houthis. Yemen has certain strategic values for both the regional powers, and clearly the involvement of the external players in Yemen conflict has affected the stability and security in the country. For Saudi Arabia, which shares a long border with Yemen, any uncontrolled turmoil in that country becomes a major security challenge.[42] Iran on the other hand can use Yemen as a strategic pawn.[43] By sympathising with the Houthis, Iran has made its posturing clear that the involvement of Saudi Arabia in Yemen is not acceptable to it. Saudi military intervention and the Iranian disapproval to it has brought to the fore the sectarian nature of the conflict. Though the sectarian dimension in the political conflict in Yemen has historical roots, the direct military involvement by Saudi Arabia and the subsequent Iranian reaction to it has further exacerbated this division.

Iran has out rightly discarded the allegations of its political and military support for the Houthis but has expressed its solidarity for the legitimate aspirations and rights of the Houthis. Iran believes that any future political roadmap of Yemen must include the Houthis. Iran, therefore, while calling for 'dialogue and reconciliation' severely condemned the Operation Decisive Storm alleging it as 'military aggression' and 'against Yemen's sovereignty'. Iranian allies in the region have also come forward condemning the coalition military operation in Yemen. Syrian regime calls the Saudi-led military operations as 'blatant aggression' on Yemen.[44] Similarly, Hezbollah condemned the military operation as 'lacking wisdom and legitimate legal reason'.[45] Hezbollah leader Hassan Nasrallah stated that Al Saud family intends to 'dominate and subjugate'.[46] Hezbollah also discards the Saudi claims of success in the military operations in Yemen stating that not a single objective was achieved by the military strikes.[47] Iraq has also expressed concern over the military intervention in Yemen and called upon the parties in Yemen for a political solution to the crisis. Iraq is of the view that military intervention hinders the prospects of political solutions to the conflict.[48] Iraqi Foreign Minister Ibrahim Al Jaafari categorically stated that Iraq was 'against foreign intervention'.[49] Prime Minister Haider Al Abadi asserted that there was 'no logic' in the Saudi-led military intervention and that the 'problem of Yemen is within Yemen'.[50]

Iran has been able to exert considerable pressure on the Saudi-led military strikes through its allies in the region. The regional geopolitical faultlines are clearly discernible in Yemen at present. Though the allegations and refusal of Iranian backing of the Houthi rebels continue, the existence of deep political divisions have come out in the open. Thus, as the coalition military strikes against the Houthis continue, the rebels continue to get the backing of Iran and its allies in the region which would provide significant moral support to sustain their activities. In April 2015, Iranian Foreign Minister Javad Zarif visited Oman and Pakistan – two countries who refused to participate the Saudi-led Operation Decisive Storm in Yemen. Zarif was in Pakistan in April 2015 and met Prime Minister Sharif and Army Chief Raheel Sharif. The two sides reportedly discussed the situation in Yemen and other bilateral issues. During his visit to Oman, Zarif met with the Omani Foreign Minister Yusuf bin Alawi and expressed his appreciation of the Omani position on Yemen. By visiting these two countries and discussing regional and bilateral issues with them Iran was trying to keep them as far as possible from the Saudi-led military coalition in Yemen.

Several allegations have been made by a number of countries

regarding the Iranian support to the Houthis. In April 2015, US Secretary of State John Kerry warned that the US would not "stand by while the region is destabilized, or while people engage in overt warfare across lines – international boundaries of other countries."[51] Saudi Arabia has made severe allegations against Iran of supporting the Houthis with money and weapons. In April 2015, Adel Al Jubeir, the then Saudi Ambassador to the US, stated that "Iran provides financial support for the Houthis, helps them build weapon factories, and gives them weapons."[52] He added that there were Iranians present in Yemen who were working alongside the Houthis. In September 2015, the Saudi-led coalition claimed that it had seized an Iranian vessel off the Omani coast with weapons, which was heading for Houthis in Yemen. The seized weapons included 'eight anti-armoured Concourse shells, 54 anti-tank BGM17 shells, 15 shell battery kits, four firing guidance systems, five binocular batteries, three launchers, one launchers' holder and three batteries.'[53] The coalition claimed that the boat was registered as a fishing boat. Again in March 2016, the US Navy seized another Iranian boat loaded with weapons. The weapons included 1,500 AK-47s, 200 RPG launchers and 21 .50-calibre machine guns.[54] Iran on its part denies all such allegations.

American Involvement

The US has been a key external player in Yemen. The primary interest of the US in Yemen has been to contain the activities of Al-Qaeda which has found a safe haven in the country. For the US, Yemen is strategically important country for the stability of the Arabian Peninsula. An unstable Yemen would pose further security challenges such as illegal migration, smuggling and extremism for Saudi Arabia. For the US, Yemen is strategically significant for the security of Bab el-Mandeb Strait, as important chokepoint connecting the Red Sea with the Gulf of Aden and the Arabian Sea.[55] This route is especially important for the shipping of millions of barrels of crude oil to various parts of the world.

The Saleh government was not able to tackle the growth and activities of Al-Qaeda. AQAP was a threat for the American interests in the region, including the Gulf States. As the Saleh regime was both financially and militarily weak to fight against Al-Qaeda's deeply entrenched network in Yemen, Saleh sought help and support from the US. The successive US presidents have collaborated with the Saleh regime to deal with the AQAP. Therefore, Yemen has been receiving huge amount of aid from the US to deal with terror.

Historically, Yemen did not have cordial relations with the US. Though the US established diplomatic relations with North Yemen in 1946,[56] it did not have much economic interest or strategic content in the relationship. The major turn in the US-Yemen relationship came only after the unification of Yemen in 1990. This coincided with the end of the Cold War and fall of the Soviet Union, which had a significant influence on the South Yemen. But immediately after Yemen unification, the 1991 Gulf War came to be another hurdle in the relationship as president Saleh supported Saddam Hussein's invasion of Kuwait. Yemen was then a non-permanent member of the UN Security Council and it opposed the UNSC resolutions condemning Saddam Hussein's actions.[57] Through the late 1990s the US received several terrorist threats originating from Yemen. The relationship bore further strain after Al-Qaeda attacked *USS Cole* in Aden in 2000. The US then came to realise that Al-Qaeda was a threat to its interest in Yemen. Until then the US-Yemeni relationship did not take deep root. The US had not heavily invested on Yemen nor did Yemen believe that US could be a benefactor.[58] The *USS Cole* attack was an important incident for the US to rethink about its approach towards Yemen. A series of other terrorist attacks took place in Yemen and it was also disclosed that an international network of terrorists operated from Yemen. President Saleh visited the US in November 2001 and US Vice-President Dick Cheney visited Yemen in March 2002. The military cooperation grew and Yemen, over the years, has received millions of dollars of aid and assistance from the US. The 9/11 attacks further consolidated such perception, thereby leading to strengthening of the US-Yemen security and military partnership targeted to fight terror. Al-Qaeda's activities gradually increased in Yemen. The Saleh regime lacked political will, financial resources and military capabilities to fight Al-Qaeda. The organisation slowly spread its tentacles and launched several attacks on the neighbouring Saudi Arabia. In the Khobar Towers attacks by Al-Qaeda in 1996 in Dhahran in Saudi Arabia, as many as 19 US military personnel were killed and many others were injured.

Saleh, as a partner in anti-terror operations, received huge sums of American aid. The US has also been giving aid to Yemen for social and humanitarian purposes. On August 4, 2014, the State Department stated that US assistance to Yemen had crossed US$ 800 million since the beginning of transition in November 2011. The US provides assistance for economic growth, social welfare, humanitarian assistance and supporting security. Between November 2011 through August 2014, Yemen received US$ 275 million for counterterrorism capacity building of Yemeni security forces, countering violent extremism and for criminal justice reform.[59] Earlier, from 2006 to 2009, the US provided US$ 97.3 million[60] under Section 1206 of the National Defense Authorization Act (NDAA).[61] Similarly, US Foreign Military Financing (FMF)[62] to Yemen has increased significantly since 2011. From 2002 to 2009, the US FMF to Yemen was US$ 71 million.[63] Since 2010 till 2015, FMF has increased substantially to reach US$ 116.44 million.[64]

The US has launched drone attacks on Al-Qaeda targets in Yemen. Without putting boots on the ground, the US has been conducting counterterrorism operations in Yemen by using unmanned aerial vehicles since 2002.[65] Such operations have significantly increased in the aftermath of the protests in 2011 when Al-Qaeda, taking opportunity of the prevailing chaos, spread its activities and captured many cities as well. Then President Obama preferred deploying drones as a useful method of countering Al-Qaeda in Yemen. According to the *Long War Journal*, till May 2016, the US has carried out 145 drone strikes in Yemen, which killed 735 terrorists and 105 civilians.[66] A large number of Yemeni citizens view the frequent drone strikes as an excessive response by the US; and Al-Qaeda is trying to exploit that sentiment by disseminating misperceptions of American power and, at the same time, 'offering an alternative route to justice and empowerment'.[67] From the beginning, the Houthis have protested against American interference in Yemen and the Saleh regime's close relationship with the US. Anti-Americanism has been a key agenda of the Houthis. The suspected nexus of Houthis with Iran also puts the US in wary. President Hadi's alliance with Saudi Arabia and the US further exposes the sectarian divide in the politics of Yemen. As the Houthis and Al-Qaeda also fight between themselves the conflict in Yemen transforms itself into a full-blown sectarian one. The situation continues to unfold and the role of US remains vital in the future political and security environment of Yemen. On the political and diplomatic front, the US has been playing a crucial role since the transition process started in Yemen. The US supported the GCC Initiative which led to Saleh stepping down as President. It played an instrumental role in the NDC by providing technical assistance for organising the dialogue. US policy in Yemen is intended to achieve a peaceful transition in the country which will enable it to maintain its counterterrorism operations to tackle the menace of Al-Qaeda. Its policy also aims at securing the interests of its allies in the neighbourhood such as Saudi Arabia and other GCC countries during the turbulent period in Yemen.[68] But as the instability continues with Al-Qaeda and Houthis growing because of the poor response from the state, US will continue to face challenges in Yemen in the foreseeable future.

The UN and the Crisis in Yemen

The UN has been watching the developments in Yemen with serious concern. It has made several appeals for peace, stability and cessation of hostilities by the parties. There have been a number of external players such as Saudi Arabia, GCC, Iran, US and so on who have intervened in the Yemeni conflict; but the UN remains the only international actor who has earned legitimacy and credibility among all the political parties and groups, even the groups most sensitive to external intervention.[69] With the conflict escalating, the UN appointed Jamal Benomar as Special Adviser to Yemen in April 2011 to guide the country through a peaceful transition. He made efforts for negotiation among the fighting Yemeni groups as per the GCC Initiative and the Implementation Mechanism. He was also seen as instrumental in holding the NDC by bringing all the factions together. But he resigned in April 2015, after violence continued to escalate throughout the country and the outcomes of the NDC were not adhered to by the parties. Besides, the Saudi-led coalition's military strikes on Yemen led to further instability.

In April 2015, UN Secretary General Ban Ki-moon appointed Ismail Ould Cheikh Ahmed of Mauritania as his Special Envoy to Yemen. He was mandated to 'work closely with the members of the United Nations Security Council, the Gulf Cooperation Council, Governments in the region and other partners, as well as the United Nations Country Team for Yemen'.[70] Ahmed convened peace talks in Geneva in June 2015. But the talks failed as the Houthis refused to meet the government delegation.[71] Also, the disagreement over main issues persisted in the minds of the delegations before they could sit together for a negotiation. While the government side demanded that the Houthis withdraw from the areas they had captured, the Houthis demanded an end to air strikes by the government as well as by the Saudi-led coalition forces.[72] This led to the collapse of the Geneva talks. A second round of talks took place at Magglingen in Switzerland in December 2015. The talks were intended to bring cessation to the hostilities and to bring a peaceful transition in the country as per the GCC Initiative, Implementation Mechanism and the NDC outcomes. The talks also discussed 'humanitarian issues, confidence-building measures and a general framework that could serve as the foundation for a comprehensive settlement.'[73] A ceasefire was declared by the UN on December 15, 2015, but heavy violations were reported throughout the country. After several attempts the UN was able to bring the government and the opposing factions to the table for further negotiations in Kuwait. But the talks in Kuwait also did not help to bring any solution and it ended inconclusively.

On April 14, 2015, UN adopted resolution 2216 on Yemen. Among others, the resolution: (i) declared Hadi as the legitimate President of the country; (ii) notedhis formal request to the GCC countries to intervene in Yemen by all means, including the use of force to deter the Houthis; (iii) called upon all the Yemeni parties to refrain from unilateral action; (iv) urged the Houthis to refrain from all violent activities; (v) asked the Houthis to withdraw from the areas they had captured; (vi) called upon all the Yemeni parties to abide by the GCC Initiative and the Implementation Mechanism, and the outcomes of the NDC; (vii) imposed an arms embargo on Yemen and allowed Yemen's neighbouring states to inspect any cargo heading to Yemen suspected of containing weapons, ammunition or military equipment; and (viii) imposed sanctions on the people who were believed to be threats to peace and stability in the country such as Saleh and Houthi leader Abdul Malik Al Houthi.[74] These restrictions include freezing of their financial assets and travel ban.

Iran has called upon the UN to urge the coalition to stop military attacks and instead work in the way of preventing further damage to Yemen. Foreign Minister Mohammad Javad Zarif appealed to the UN Secretary General to stop the 'genocide' and 'end the crimes against the people of Yemen.'[75] Iran has expressed the belief that the Saudi-led military strikes in Yemen are against international norms and has called for an active contribution from the UN to expedite humanitarian aid to reach the Yemeni people.[76] In April 2015, Foreign Minister Javad Zarif, in a letter to the Security Council, proposed a four-point formula to address the conflict in Yemen. They are: (i) ceasefire and an immediate end to all foreign military attacks; (ii) unimpeded urgent humanitarian and medical assistance to the people of Yemen; (iii) resumption of Yemeni-led and Yemeni-owned national dialogue, with the participation of the representatives of all political parties and social groups; and (iv) establishment of an inclusive national unity government. Zarif also stated that the only way to restore peace and stability in Yemen was 'to allow all Yemeni parties to establish, without any foreign interference, their own inclusive national unity government.'[77]

In April 2016, the conflicting parties of Yemen agreed to a ceasefire prior to the UN-mediated peace talks in Kuwait. The Houthis and the Hadi government agreed to participate in the talks. The objective of the talks was to 'reach a comprehensive agreement that lays the foundations for a return to a peaceful and orderly transition based on the GCC Initiative and its Implementation Mechanism' and the outcome of the NDC.[78] Though there were initial allegations of ceasefire violations by both the sides, they resumed the talks under UN mediation. A De-escalation and Co-ordination Committee (DCC) comprising military representatives from both sides was formed to look after the ceasefire. The DCC was also assigned the task of investigating the clashes on the ground and to provide the 'UN with detailed reports with the aim of protecting the on-going peace talks from daily developments on the ground.'[79] The UN maintains regular contacts with the DCC to 'investigate and halt all breaches of the cessation of hostilities.'[80] The UN Secretary General's Special Envoy, Ismail Ould Cheikh Ahmed, stated that the talks would focus on five crucial issues: (i) the withdrawal of militias and armed groups; (ii) the handover of heavy weapons to the State; (iii) interim security arrangements; (iv) the restoration of state institutions and the resumption of inclusive political dialogue; and (v) the creation of a special committee for prisoners and detainees.[81] But on August 6, 2016, he announced the end of the peace talks citing lack of trust between the parties and the unilateral actions from both sides.[82]

Al-Qaeda and ISIS Gaining Ground

Yemen has been a safe haven for Al-Qaeda and the organisation in running AQAP from Yemen. It has capitalised on the protracted conflict and weaknesses of the state military apparatus in Yemen to grow and expand its activities. After the protests started against the Saleh regime in 2011, Al-Qaeda captured a large number of cities in Yemen while the security forces were deployed in many places to control the protesters. Al-Qaeda's dominant presence has been seen in the south of the country in provinces such as Abyan, Zinjibar, Hadramaut, Exploiting the instability, they have expanded their area to other parts of the country as well. The sudden spurt in territorial offensive launched by Al-Qaeda seems a conscious decision on their part to step up attacks to seize the opportunity created by the Arab Spring.[83] Al-Qaeda seems to be taking advantage of the fighting between the state forces alongside the coalition forces against the Houthis. According to one report, Al-Qaeda now runs a mini-state in the Yemeni port city of Muqalla and it has reportedly looted the Mukalla central bank branch of an estimated US$ 100 million. It is also estimated that Al-Qaeda in Yemen has extorted US$ 1.4 million from the national oil company and collects up to US$ 2 million every day in taxes on goods and fuel coming into the port.[84] Another disturbing trend is that the organisation is sympathising itself with the Southerners in Yemen who complain of being marginalised by the government.

Yemen has faced a resource crunch to effectively fight Al-Qaeda. The military has also remained ill prepared to defeat it. The capture of Sanaa by the Houthis has further aggravated the situation. While the security forces are engaged with the Houthis to recapture the capital, Al-Qaeda continues to gain territories almost effortlessly. Al-Qaeda has undertaken a serious campaign of launching terrorist attacks on Yemen's security and intelligence personnel, army units, and tribal and community leaders who cooperate with the government.[85] Besides, Al-Qaeda is exploiting the existing insecurity and erosion of government services to win the goodwill and support of the local people.[86] Despite the Saudi claims of killing 800 Al-Qaeda terrorists in Muqalla,[87] Al-Qaeda has captured five other cities, as follows: Houta, the capital of Lahej province, Azzan in Shabwa, Mahfid, Shoqra and Ahwar in Abyan province.[88]

Another disturbing trend that is challenging Yemeni security is the emergence and steady consolidation of ISIS in the country. Besides Al-Qaeda's growing activities, the faltering Yemeni state also faces the wrath of the growing ISIS. Like Al-Qaeda, the ISIS has also taken the opportunity of the existing lawlessness and weak security apparatus in the country. The emergence of ISIS in Yemen has added yet another dimension to the existing chaos in the conflict ridden Yemen. Over last few years ISIS has launched several attacks killing many people, including Jaafar Mohamed Saad, the governor of Aden. ISIS has been targeting Shia mosques, government officials, security forces, and the coalition forces. It has tried to carve out a territory for itself but without much success. But it has been able to build a training camp for its combatants in Lahej.[89]

Humanitarian Crisis

The humanitarian situation in Yemen has 'drastically deteriorated'.[90] A large number of people are in dire need of basic services such as food, water and medicine. According to the United Nations Office for the Coordination of Humanitarian Affairs (UNOCHA), more than 2.5 million people have been internally displaced and around 14.4 million are food-insecure. The number of internally displaced people has increased by four times since the beginning of 2015. UNOCHA also estimates that there is one-third increase in the number of people requiring some form of humanitarian or protection assistance since the situation escalated in March 2015. Around 21.2 million people, about 82 percent of the population of the country, need such assistance.[91] Similarly, there has been a visible increase in the number of civilian casualties in the country since the beginning of the coalition strike. Saudi Arabia has established a committee to look into the alleged human rights violations.

Yemen is one of the economically underdeveloped countries in the West Asian region. Around 80 percent of the national income comes from petroleum resources, which are rapidly depleting. More than half of the population does not have access to clean drinking water. Health, education, food security, malnourishment, etc. are the basic issues which have been haunting the country.[92] The widespread violence and killings witnessed in the country since the beginning of the Arab Spring has further deteriorated the situation. It is difficult to obtain data on gender based violence in the conflict situation but the vulnerability of women to abuse and exploitation increases significantly during a situation of internal strife as the protection system has completely broken down in the country. Also, in a number of cases, the male members of the families have left home to join the fighting, thereby leaving the women at home or displaced.[93]

Into the Future

The situation in Yemen continues to unfold with continuing violence and uncertain political developments. Thousands of people have been killed, millions have become internally displaced and in dire need of humanitarian assistance. The path to transition has been unreasonably protracted and turbulent. Saleh's ouster was a moment of opportunity for the Yemenis to make a fresh beginning, moving away from authoritarianism. The GCC Initiative was the right platform for a smooth transition and the holding of the NDC was a step in the right direction. But the lack of trust among the political parties and other stakeholders in the country, intervention by external powers, spurt in violence, etc. have not allowed peace to settle. During the NDC, the Houthis and the Southerners were vocal in putting forward their demands and withdrew if their demands were not accepted. The Houthis' march to Sanaa, Hadi's house arrest, seizure of the presidential palace etc. completely derailed the process of transition.

The Houthi capture of Sanaa was a red line for Saudi Arabia to accept. It immediately formed a military coalition and started military operation to push the Houthis back to Saada. This has been yet another roadblock for Yemen's transition process. The Saudi-led military operation has not been able to bring Hadi back to power nor has it been able to completely drive the Houthis out of the capital. Saudi Arabia appears to be more concerned about its own national security challenges and losing regional influence in the Gulf than about Yemen's stability. Iran on its part wants to capitalise upon the chaos. Both Iran and Saudi Arabia have brought in their allies and friends to support their moves, making the situation more complex. The Saudi-led operation has further exposed the deep political and sectarian polarisation in Yemen in particular and in the region in general. While the Hadi-led forces and his other forces fighting with him are getting full political and military support from Saudi Arabia, Houthis are getting political support from Iran though the Iranian military support to them remains unclear. The activities of both these regional players, Iran and Saudi Arabia will, to a large extent, determine the peace, stability and transition in Yemen. While both the regional powers vie for power and influence, Yemenis continue to suffer and the country seems to be slipping in to further instability.

END NOTES

1. For a discussion on tribalism in Yemen see Nadwa Al Dawsari, "Tribal governance and stability in Yemen", The Carnegie Papers, April 2012, at http://carnegieendowment.org/2012/04/24/tribal-governance-and-stability-in-yemen.
2. Ahmad Ali Al Ahsab, "What makes Yemen's spring different?", in John Davis (ed.), *The Arab Spring and Arab Thaw: Unfinished Revolutions and the Quest for Democracy*, Routledge, New York, 2013, pp. 45-50.
3. For a detailed study, see Falah Al Mdaires, "Political Islamic movements in modern Yemen", *Journal of South Asian and Middle Eastern Studies*, 24 (2), 2001, pp. 73-86.
4. Farea Al Muslimi, "How Sunni Shia Sectarianism is Poisoning Yemen", Carnegie Endowment for International Peace, at http://carnegieendowment.org/syriaincrisis/?fa=62375.

5. "Top army commanders defect in Yemen", *Al Jazeera*, March 21, 2011, at http://www.aljazeera.com/news/middleeast/2011/03/2011320180579476.html.
6. Michael Knights, "The military role in Yemen's protests: civil-military relations in the tribal republic", *Journal of Strategic Studies*, 36 (2), 2013, p. 278.
7. Farea Al Muslimi, "How Sunni Shia sectarianism is poisoning Yemen", Carnegie Endowment for International Peace, at http://carnegieendowment.org/syriaincrisis/?fa=62375.
8. Ginny Hill and Gerd Nonneman, "Yemen, Saudi Arabia, and the Gulf states: Elite politics, street protests and regional diplomacy", Royal Institute of International Affairs, May 12, 2011, at https://www.chathamhouse.org/sites/files/chathamhouse/public/Meetings/Meeting%20Transcripts/120511yemen.pdf.
9. "Yemen parliament approves immunity law", *Al Jazeera*, January 21, 2012, at http://www.aljazeera.com/news/middleeast/2012/01/201212064413492432.html
10. "Yemeni parliament grants President Saleh full immunity from prosecution", *Al Arabiya*, January 21, 2012, at https://english.alarabiya.net/articles/2012/01/21/189609.html.
11. "Yemen: Reject immunity law for President Saleh and aides", Human Rights Watch, January 10, 2012, at https://www.hrw.org/news/2012/01/10/yemen-reject-immunity-law-president-saleh-and-aides.
12. "Yemen: Immunity law deals blow to victims of abuses", Amnesty International, January 24, 2012, at http://www.amnesty.org.au/news/comments/27686/.
13. Hill and Nonneman, n. 8.
14. Charles Schmitz, "Yemen's National Dialogue", *Middle East Institute Policy Paper 2014-1*, February 2014, at http://www.mei.edu/sites/default/files/publications/Charles%20Schmitz%20Policy%20Paper.pdf.
15. See the full text of the GCC initiative, "Agreement on the implementation mechanism for the transition process in Yemen in accordance with the initiative of the Gulf Cooperation Council (GCC)", May 12, 2011, at http://peacemaker.un.org/sites/peacemaker.un.org/files/YE_111205_Agreement%20on%20the%20implementation%20mechanism%20for%20the%20transition.pdf.
16. Erica Gaston, "Process lessons learned in Yemen's National Dialogue", *USIP Special Report 342*, February 2014, at http://www.usip.org/sites/default/files/SR342_Process-Lessons-Learned-in-Yemens-National-Dialogue.pdf, accessed on December 2, 2014. See the details of the NDC's topics and subtopics at http://www.ndc.ye/page.aspx?show=67.
17. "Yemen's national dialogue conference concludes with agreement", *BBC News*, January 21, 2014, at http://www.bbc.com/news/world-middle-east-25835721.
18. "Shia rebels, southern group slam Yemen federation plan", *The Peninsula*, February 12, 2014, at http://thepeninsulaqatar.com/news/middle-east/272137/shia-rebels-southern-group-slam-yemen-federation-plan.
19. "Yemen's Houthi rebels announce government takeover", *The Guardian*, February 6, 2015, http://www.theguardian.com/world/2015/feb/06/yemen-houthi-dissolves-parliament.
20. For a discussion on Houthis and Zaidism, see Lucas Winter, "Conflict in Yemen: simple people, complicated circumstances", *Middle East Policy*, 18 (1), Spring 2011, pp. 102-120.

21. "What is the Houthi movement?", *Religion and Politics*, September 7, 2016, at http://www.religionandgeopolitics.org/houthi-movement/what-houthi-movement.
22. "Yemen crisis: Houthi rebels are Iran stooges, says Hadi", *BBC News*, March 29, 2015, at http://www.bbc.com/news/world-middle-east-32098607.
23. "The Huthis: From Saada to Sanaa", International Crisis Group, Middle East Report No. 154, June 10, 2014, at http://www.crisisgroup.org/~/media/Files/Middle%20East%20North%20Africa/Iran%20Gulf/Yemen/154-the-huthis-from-saada-to-sanaa.pdf.
24. "Houthi-Salafi conflict rages on in northern Yemen", *Al Khabar*, October 31, 2013, at http://english.al-akhbar.com/node/17472.
25. "Yemen deploys troops to monitor ceasefire", *Al Jazeera*, January 11, 2014, at http://www.aljazeera.com/news/middleeast/2014/01/yemen-deploys-troops-monitor-ceasefire-20141115321289045б.html.
26. Thomas Juneau, "Yemen and Arab Spring: Elite struggles, State collapse and regional security", *Orbis*, 57 (3), 2013, p. 411.
27. Ibid., p. 419.
28. William A. Rugh, "Problems in Yemen, domestic and foreign", *Middle East Policy*, 22 (4), Winter 2015, p. 146; Noel Brehony, "Yemen and the Huthis: Genesis of the 2015 crisis", *Asian Affairs*, 46 (2), 2015, pp. 240-241.
29. "Yemen: Is peace possible?", International Crisis Group, Middle East Report No. 167, February 9, 2016, at http://www.crisisgroup.org/~/media/Files/Middle%20East%20North%20Africa/Iran%20Gulf/Yemen/167-yemen-is-peace-possible.pdf.
30. F. Gregory Gause III, "Saudi Arabia's regional security strategy", in Mehran Kamrava (ed.), *The International Politics of the Persian Gulf*, Syracuse University Press, Syracuse, 2011, pp. 169-183; Khaled Fattah, "Yemen: A social intifada in a republic of sheikhs", *Middle East Policy*, 18 (3), Fall 2011, p. 83.
31. Maria Louise Clausen, "Understanding the crisis in Yemen: Evaluating competing narratives", *The International Spectator*, 50 (3), 2015, p. 20.
32. Peter Salisbury, "Yemen and the Saudi–Iranian 'Cold War'", The Royal Institute of International Affairs, February 2015, at https://www.chathamhouse.org/sites/files/chathamhouse/field/field_document/20150218YemenIranSaudi.pdf.
33. Stig Stenslie, "Not too strong, not too weak: Saudi Arabia's policy towards Yemen", The Norwegian Peacebuilding Resource Centre, Issue Brief, March 2013, at http://www.peacebuilding.no/var/ezflow_site/storage/original/application/87736bc4da8b0e482f9492e6e8baacaf.pdf.
34. "Yemen combatants not ready for talks, says neighbour Oman", *Reuters*, April 2, 2015, at http://in.reuters.com/article/yemen-security-oman-idINKBN0MT22X20150402.
35. For more on Ibadi Islam see Valerie J. Hoffman, *The Essentials of Ibadi Islam*, Syracuse University Press, Syracuse, 2012; and Hussein Ghubas, *Oman – The Islamic Democratic Tradition*, Routledge, New York, 2006.
36. Prasanta Kumar Pradhan, "Operation Decisive Storm and changing geopolitics in the Gulf", IDSA Issue Brief, May 26, 2015, at http://www.idsa.in/issuebrief/OperationDecisiveStorm_pkpradhan_260515#footnoteref3_1m1x1yw.
37. "Operation 'Decisive Storm' ends, what's next?", *SUSTG*, April 21, 2015, at

http://susris.com/2015/04/21/special-report-operation-decisive-storm-ends-whats-next/.

38. Amir Sajedi, "Yemen crisis in the regional context", *Iranian Review of Foreign Affairs*, 5 (3), Fall 2014, pp. 65-85; W. Andrew Terrill, "Iranian involvement in Yemen", *Orbis*, 58 (3), 2014, p. 435.
39. "A former Houthi leader disclosed an Iranian plan to establish a Shiite state between KSA and Yemen; warns of possible chaos works during pilgrimage (Hajj)", *Yemen Post*, April 10, 2010, at http://yemenpost.net/Detail123456789.aspx?ID=3&SubID=1554&MainCat=3.
40. "Yemen says Iran funding rebels", *Al Jazeera*, November 16, 2009, at http://www.aljazeera.com/news/middleeast/2009/11/2009111675649700628.html.
41. Prasanta Kumar Pradhan, "Houthis and external intervention in Yemen", IDSA Comment, November 25, 2009, at http://www.idsa.in/idsacomments/HouthisandexternalinterventioninYemen_pkpradhan_251109#.
42. Salisbury, "Yemen and the Saudi–Iranian 'Cold War'", n. 32.
43. Mohsen Milani, "Iran's game in Yemen: Why Tehran isn't to blame for the civil war", *Foreign Affairs*, April 15, 2015, at https://www.foreignaffairs.com/articles/iran/2015-04-19/irans-game-yemen.
44. "Syrian Media: Saudi-led Yemen action is "blatant aggression"", *Reuters*, March 26, 2015, at http://www.reuters.com/article/yemen-security-syria-idUSL6N0WS4AT20150326.
45. "Hezbollah condemns military intervention in Yemen", *Lebanon News*, March 27, 2015, at http://www.lebanonnews.net/index.php/sid/231423513.
46. "Nasrallah: Saudi aggression on Yemen an attempt to dominate and subjugate it", March 27, 2015, *Syrian Arab News Agency*, at http://sana.sy/en/?p=33695.
47. "Saudi war on Yemen has failed: Hezbollah chief", *Press TV*, May 5, 2015, at http://www.presstv.ir/Detail/2015/05/05/409623/Hezbollah-Nasrallah-yemen-Saudiaggression-Houthi.
48. Ministry of Foreign Affairs, Government of Iraq, "Statement on the Developments in Yemen", March 26, 2015, at http://www.mofa.gov.iq/en/news/statement-on-the-developments-in-yemen.
49. "Iraq opposes Saudi-led air strikes in Yemen: FM", *Al Manar*, March 26, 2105, at http://www.almanar.com.lb/english/adetails.php?eid=203014&frid=23&seccatid=24&cid=23&fromval=1
50. "Tensions flare between Iraq and Saudi Arabia in U.S. coalition", *The New York Times*, April 15, 2015, at http://www.nytimes.com/2015/04/16/world/middleeast/iraqi-prime-minister-criticizes-saudi-intervention-in-yemen.html?_r=1
51. "Kerry says U.S. knew of Iran's military aid to Houthi rebels", *New York Times*, April 9, 2015, at http://www.nytimes.com/2015/04/10/world/middleeast/kerry-us-iran-military-aid-houthi-yemen.html?_r=0.
52. "Iran supporting Houthis 'with arms and money'", *Arab News*, April 8, 2015, at http://www.arabnews.com/saudi-arabia/news/729476.
53. "'Caught red-handed': Coalition says it seized Iran boat with arms for Yemen rebels", *Gulf News*, September 30, 2015, at http://gulfnews.com/news/mena/iran/caught-red-handed-coalition-says-it-seized-iran-boat-with-arms-for-yemen-rebels-1.1592623.

54. "Third illicit arms shipment in recent weeks seized in Arabian Sea", USA Navy, April 4, 2016, at http://www.navy.mil/submit/display.asp?story_id=93990.
55. Anthony H. Cordesman, "America, Saudi Arabia, and the strategic importance of Yemen", Centre for Strategic and International Studies, March 26, 2015, at http://csis.org/publication/america-saudi-arabia-and-strategic-importance-yemen.
56. For a discussion of the history of US-Yemen relations, see Ahmed Noman Kassim Almadhagi, *Yemen and the USA: A Super-Power and a Small-state Relationship, 1962-1992*, I.B. Tauris, London, 1996.
57. J.E. Peterson, "The United States and Yemen: A history of unfulfilled expectations", in Robert E. Looney (ed.), *Handbook of US-Middle East Relations: Formative Factors and Regional Perspectives*, Routledge, London, 2009, p. 504.
58. Sheila Carapico, "No quick fix: foreign aid and state performance in Yemen", in Nancy Birdsall, Milan Vaishnav and Robert L. Ayers (eds.), *Short of the Goal: US Policy and Poorly Performing States*, Centre for Global Development, Washington D.C., p. 185.
59. "U.S. Support for Yemen", *US Department of State Fact Sheet*, August 4, 2014, at http://www.state.gov/p/nea/rls/2014/222781.htm.
60. "Following the money in Yemen and Lebanon: Maximizing the effectiveness of U.S. security assistance and international financial institution lending", Committee on Foreign Relations, United States Senate, Washington DC, January 5, 2010, at http://www.foreign.senate.gov/imo/media/doc/54245.pdf.
61. Section 1206 of the National Defense Authorization Act (NDAA) of the US provides the Secretary of Defense with authority to train and equip foreign military forces for two specified purposes—counterterrorism and stability operations—and foreign security forces for counterterrorism operations. For details, see Nina M. Serafino, "Security Assistance Reform: 'Section 1206': background and issues for Congress", Congressional Research Service, December 8, 2014, at https://www.fas.org/sgp/crs/natsec/RS22855.pdf.
62. According to the Defense Security Cooperation Agency, under the FMF, assistance is provided to partner countries to purchase US defence articles, services and training. While the Secretary of State determines the eligibility of the countries for the programme, it is the Secretary of Defense who executes the program.
63. "Following the money in Yemen and Lebanon...", n. 60.
64. See the "Foreign Military Financing Account Summary", US Department of State, at http://www.state.gov/t/pm/ppa/sat/c14560.htm.
65. For a detailed discussion of US drone strikes in Yemen, see Leila Hudson, Colin S. Owens and David J. Callen, "Drone warfare in Yemen: fostering emirates through counterterrorism?", *Middle East Policy*, 19 (3), Fall 2012, pp. 142-156.
66. Bill Roggio and Bob Barry, "Charting the data for US air strikes in Yemen, 2002–2016", *The Long War Journal*, May 10, 2016, at http://www.longwarjournal.org/multimedia/Yemen/code/Yemen-strike.php.
67. Jillian Schwedler, "Is the U.S. drone program in Yemen working?", Brookings Institution, September 28, 2015, at http://www.brookings.edu/blogs/markaz/posts/2015/09/29-us-drone-program-yemen.
68. "United States policy & Yemen's armed conflict", The Yemen Peace Project,

September 2015, at http://www.yemenpeaceproject.org/wp-content/uploads/2015/08/US-Policy-and-Yemens-Armed-Conflict.pdf.

69. Ibrahim Sharqieh, "A lasting peace? Yemen's long journey to national reconciliation", Brookings Doha Center Analysis Paper, No. 7, February 2013, p. 21, at http://www.brookings.edu/~/media/Research/Files/Papers/2013/02/11%20yemen%20national%20reconciliation%20sharqieh/BDC_Yemen%20National%20Reconciliation_Sharqieh.pdf.
70. "Secretary-General appoints Ismail Ould Cheikh Ahmed of Mauritania as his Special Envoy for Yemen", UN Press Release, April 25, 2015, at http://www.un.org/press/en/2015/sga1563.doc.htm.
71. "Yemen peace talks in Geneva collapse", *Al Jazeera*, June 15, 2015, at http://www.aljazeera.com/news/2015/06/yemen-peace-talks-geneva-collapse-150619122221975.html.
72. "Yemen crisis: Geneva talks fail to produce ceasefire", *BBC News*, June 19, 2015, at http://www.bbc.com/news/world-middle-east-33205359.
73. Briefing by UN special envoy to Yemen Ismail Ould Cheikh Ahmed at the United Nations Security Council 7596th meeting, December 22, 2015, at http://www.securitycouncilreport.org/atf/cf/%7B65BFCF9B-6D27-4E9C-8CD3-CF6E4FF96FF9%7D/s_pv_7596.pdf.
74. United Nations Security Council Resolution 2216 (2015), Adopted by the Security Council on April 14, 2015, at http://www.un.org/en/ga/search/view_doc.asp?symbol=S/RES/2216(2015).
75. "Iranian Foreign Minister urges UN to check Yemen aggression", Ministry of Foreign Affairs, Islamic Republic of Iran, May 12, 2015, at http://en.mfa.ir/index.aspx?siteid=3&pageid=2030&newsview=340382&pro=nobak.
76. "Afkham: Saudi genocide in Yemen is against international norms", Ministry of Foreign Affairs, Islamic Republic of Iran, May 10, 2015, at http://en.mfa.ir/index.aspx?siteid=3&pageid=2021&newsview=340095&pro=nobak.
77. "Annex to the letter dated 17 April 2015 from the Permanent Representative of the Islamic Republic of Iran to the United Nations addressed to the Secretary-General, United Nations Security Council", April 17, 2015, at http://www.securitycouncilreport.org/atf/cf/%7B65BFCF9B-6D27-4E9C-8CD3-CF6E4FF96FF9%7D/s_2015_263.pdf.
78. "Statement of UN Special Envoy for Yemen, Ismail Ould Cheikh Ahmed – First Press Conference on peace talks in the State of Kuwait", United Nations, April 22, 2016, at http://www.un.org/sg/offthecuff/index.asp?nid=4495.
79. "Yemen: UN-mediated peace talks continuing amid 'worrying' breaches of the cessation of hostilities", UN News Centre, May 5, 2016, at http://www.un.org/apps/news/story.asp?NewsID=53866#.
80. "Despite 'positive atmosphere,' Government of Yemen suspends participation from joint peace talks", UN News Centre, May 1, 2016, at http://www.un.org/apps/news/story.asp?NewsID=53829#.Vy28smR96rc.
81. "Yemen: UN officials welcome cessation of hostilities", UN News Centre, April 11, 2016, at http://www.un.org/apps/news/story.asp?NewsID=53650#.Vy3Eq2R96rd.
82. "UN: Yemen talks in Kuwait end, peace efforts to continue", *Al Arabiya*, August 6, 2016, at http://english.alarabiya.net/en/News/middle-east/2016/08/06/

Houthis-name-governing-body-in-Yemen.html.

83. Katherine Zimmerman, "Al-Qaeda in Yemen: Countering the Threat from the Arabian Peninsula", *Critical Threats*, October 2012, at http://www.criticalthreats.org/yemen/zimmerman-qaeda-yemen-countering-threat-arabian-peninsula-october-19-2012.
84. "How Saudi Arabia's war in Yemen has made Al-Qaeda stronger – and richer", *Reuters*, April 8, 2016, at http://www.reuters.com/investigates/special-report/yemen-aqap/.
85. Sami Kronenfeld and Yoel Guzansky, "Yemen: A mirror to the future of the Arab Spring", *Military and Strategic Affairs*, 6 (3), December 2014, p. 93.
86. Juneau, n. 26, p. 420.
87. "Saudi coalition claims it killed 800 al-Qaeda fighters in Yemen", *The Telegraph*, April 25, 2016, at http://www.telegraph.co.uk/news/2016/04/25/saudi-coalition-claims-it-killed-800-al-qaeda-fighters-in-yemen/.
88. Bill Roggio, "Al-Qaeda seizes more territory in southern Yemen", *Long War Journal*, February 11, 2016, at http://www.longwarjournal.org/archives/2016/02/al-qaeda-seizes-more-territory-in-southern-yemen.php.
89. Ashraf al-Falahi, "Islamic State extends its tentacles into Yemen", *Al Monitor*, November 30, 2015, at http://www.al-monitor.com/pulse/en/originals/2015/11/islamic-state-expands-yemen-qaeda-aqap.html.
90. "Yemen: UN warns humanitarian situation has deteriorated 'drastically' as conflict claims 5,700 lives", UN News Centre, November 18, 2015, at http://www.un.org/apps/news/story.asp?NewsID=52588.
91. "Crisis Overview", United Nations Office for the Coordination of Humanitarian Affairs, at http://www.unocha.org/yemen/crisis-overview.
92. Ismail Ould Cheick Ahmed and Trond Jensen, "Political transition and the humanitarian challenge in Yemen", Humanitarian Practice Network at the Overseas Development Institute, April 2014, at http://odihpn.org/wp-content/uploads/2014/04/HE_61_web.pdf.
93. "Violence, inequality plague women in conflict-ravaged Yemen", United Nations Population Fund, September 22, 2015, at http://www.unfpa.org/news/violence-inequality-plague-women-conflict-ravaged-yemen.

4

The Syrian Conundrum

The protests in Syria aggravated when four people were killed by the security forces in the city of Darra in March 2011. This incident triggered further protests throughout the country. Inspired by the developments in Tunisia and Egypt, Syrian protesters gathered to raise their voice against the Bashar Al Assad regime. Initially, the protesters demanded political reform, end to corruption, release of political prisoners, abolition of the emergency law etc. The regime adopted strong coercive measures to deal with the protesters. Along with the heavy deployment of police and the security forces, government used helicopters, tanks and artillery to disperse the protesters. Slowly, the protests continued to spread and the Assad regime responded with even stronger coercive measures. This further multiplied the popular anger against the regime and the determination of the protesters to call for the removal of Assad became stronger and more pronounced. In June 2011, Assad offered dialogue to the people in order to reach a political solution to the crisis. But it was immediately rejected by the people as it was believed to be too little too late.

The crisis in Syria is aggravating with the number of casualties and internally displaced people growing day by day. The regime has remained adamant and has clung to power despite the huge opposition from the people. Assad has also defied the appeals by several members of the international community to quit and allow a democratic system of government begin in the country. The opposition has started its own political and military campaign to remove Assad for power. In the process, the protest for change has now descended to a conflict between Assad's stubborn determination to continue in power and a fragmented opposition's struggle to overthrow him.

Sectarian divisions play an important role in the Syrian conflict. The nature of Syria's demography and governance has been a key driver of the conflict. About 74 percent of the Syrian population are Sunni Arabs, while 16 percent are other Muslims which includes the dominant Alawites, and about 10 percent of the population are Christians. The Assad family belongs to the Alawite Shias and are ruling over the country since decades. The Sunnis allege that the Alawites man the top political, bureaucratic and military leadership in the country, and the Sunnis are discriminated and neglected by the regime. There exists a deep-seated feeling of anguish among the Sunnis of the country. Syrian political system is highly centralised and power is concentrated in the hands of the president. Hafez Al Assad took over the powers of the country in a coup in 1970 and remained the president of the country till he died in 2000. His son Bashar Al Assad succeeded him in 2000. The Assad family has been the most powerful entity in the Syrian politics with the support and loyalty from the Alawite Shias.

Though the conflict started as an opposition to the Assad regime, subsequent internal and regional political and diplomatic developments have turned the conflict into predominantly sectarian in nature. The Assad regime is supported and backed by Iran. Syria and Iran enjoy a warm and cordial relationship and both are strategically important for each other. The Lebanese Hezbollah has also joined the war in favour of Assad against the opposition. As it is well known, Hezbollah is a predominantly Shia organisation and has close links with the Assad regime and Iran. Thus, the joining of the Hezbollah in the conflict to fight alongside the Assad substantiates the existence of sectarian nature of the conflict in Syria. On the other hand, the opposition forces are supported by the prominent Sunni countries such as Saudi Arabia, Qatar and others, who besides providing funding, have thrown their political and diplomatic weight behind the opposition. Saudi Arabia and Qatar have openly advocated for arming the opposition to protect themselves and fight against the regime's forces as they see no hope of a political or diplomatic solution to the conflict. The involvement of the Al-Qaeda and Muslim Brotherhood in the conflict against the regime leaves no ambiguity about the sectarian dimension of the conflict. Thus, at all levels – political, ideological and military – the sectarian dimension plays an important role. Though the sectarian dimension of the conflict is not the sole determinant of the developments in the country, it is certainly playing a crucial role in the developments taking place in Syria.

The Regime's Forces

Assad's stronghold over his military is one of the most important reasons for his survival against the fierce opposition. Military has remained a very powerful institution in Syria and the regime has used the military for its stability and survival. The trends in the Arab Spring has shown that leaders who have lost control over their military, where the top commanders have defected to the opposition, have lost power. Muammar Gaddafi in Libya, Hosni Mubarak in Egypt, Ali Abdullah Saleh in Yemen are the glaring examples who fell after a number of their senior commanders defected in favour of the opposition. But in Syria, though few senior military leaders have defected to join the opposition, the impact of that has not been too costly for Assad.

The secret of a highly disciplined and loyal military in Syria lies in the fact that a large number of the higher ranks of the military are held by the Alawites and the Baathists. The Republican Guard is mostly manned by the Alawites. The irregular armed groups known as the *Shabiha* are also fighting alongside the military further strengthening the regime's position. Most of the *Shabiha* members belong to the Alawite sect, thus further adding to the military advantage of Assad.[1] The opposition alleges that the *Shabiha* is 'manipulated by the secret intelligence apparatus' and it does the dirty job 'with no written orders so the state can deny responsibility'.[2] The continuation and aggravation of the conflict made the regime form other professional fighting units besides the regular military forces. In late 2012, the government established a National Defence Force (NDF) to fight against the opposition. It has also been reported that the Iranian and Hezbollah officials have played a key role in the formation of the NDF.[3] Since the establishment of the NDF, the *Shabiha* armed group has been accommodated into the new umbrella body.[4] There are a number of other pro-regime militia groups operating in Syria such as the Baath Battalions, the Jerusalem Brigade, the Syrian Resistance, Syrian Social Nationalist Party, and the Popular Front for the Liberation of Palestine-General Command.[5] According to Aron Lund, while the NDF is an organised network 'created through the rebranding, restructuring, and merging of local Popular Committees and other pro-Assad armed groups' all other militia groups are 'are poorly disciplined semi-criminal or sectarian gangs in civilian attire.'[6] The formation of the NDF served major purposes for Assad. As most of the fighters joined voluntarily, the fear of defection was very low. Also, the NDF which received training in guerrilla style, asymmetric and urban warfare for which even the Syrian Army was not prepared for.[7] There are also a number of elite security services who are extremely loyal to the regime and constitute both offensive and defensive forces. Importantly, there are political and ideological factors that keep these forces bind with the regime. They would fight with the regime till the end and they also feel that their fate is closely linked to the survival of the Assad regime.[8] Military and paramilitary forces play a very defining role in the present situation in Syria. The conflict has turned out to be a civil war between the regime's forces and the anti-government forces. While the government forces are trying to retain its stronghold all over the country, the anti-government forces are trying to gain new territories every day.

Hezbollah

Today, Hezbollah is a critical force not only for Syria but also for the region. It was formed by Iran and Syria in 1982 in the backdrop of Israel attack on Lebanon. It is primarily a Shia military force from Lebanon established with the main aim to resist the Israeli invasions in the region. Supported by the Iranian regime, the Hezbollah fighters were trained by the Iranian Islamic Revolutionary Guard Corps (IRGC). Hezbollah continued to thrive through the next decades getting active support from Iran and Syria. Its military power and funding has increased substantially. Some believe that Hezbollah's arsenal includes missiles and rockets as well. Support from Syria has come by the way of transit route for arms to Hezbollah, providing safe heaven for its personnel and the organisation. As one scholar notes, "Syria is the bridge through which Iran created Hezbollah. In practice, Syria was the logistical backing of Hezbollah. Hezbollah became the focal point of the connection between Syria and Iran."[9] In the past Hezbollah has been used as a proxy by Iran and Syria in their fight against Israel.

As the protests in Syria gradually transformed into a full scale civil war, it was only natural for Hezbollah to join the war in support of Assad regime. Participation of Hezbollah in the civil war further strengthened the regime's position which was facing strong armed opposition groups and extremists. Though initially Hezbollah leaders refuted the claims of the Syrian opposition about the involvement of Hezbollah in the conflict, it slowly became clear since late 2012 and early 2013 that Hezbollah fighters are actively involved fighting alongside the regime. They have now become a vital force for the Assad regime in protecting territories as well as defending the regime. In April 2013, Hezbollah chief Hassan Nasrallah confirmed that his forces are fighting in Syria,[10] and later in November 2013 stated that his forces will fight alongside Assad's forces as long as necessary.[11] Though exact number of casualties is difficult to ascertain, according to one source, between September 30, 2012, and February 16, 2016 at least 865 Hezbollah fighters were killed while fighting in Syria.[12] Another source claims that since 2013 Hezbollah has lost more than 1000 fighters in Syria.[13] But despite the losses, the support of Hezbollah for the Assad regime is a game changer in Syria. In 2013, Hezbollah helped the Assad regime to capture the border town on Qusair. Hezbollah's involvement in Syria started as a smaller scale intervention but has now grown significantly throughout the country including Damascus, Aleppo and Deir Ezzor.[14] Hezbollah along with officers from Iranian military are training the elite forces of Syria.[15] While fighting in Syria, Hezbollah has also lost some of its top commanders in the war. In May 2016, its top commander Mustafa Baddredine was killed in a fighting in Syria.

Hezbollah has reiterated its commitment for fighting against the Sunni extremists in Syria who are fighting against the Assad regime. In March 2016, Hezbollah's leader Nasrallah stated that they will keep fighting alongside Assad's forces till the forces like Islamic State of Iraq and Syria (ISIS) and Al-Qaeda are eliminated from Syria. He rejected any possibility of Hezbollah withdrawing from Syria and reiterated their commitment to Assad by saying that 'so long as we have a responsibility to be there, we will be there'.[16] Thus, the organisation expressed its unreserved commitment towards the Syrian regime and, in the process, has turned out to be a crucial factor in the dangerous sectarian fighting in Syria. As one observer notes, after joining to fight in Syria, 'Hezbollah has lost its position as one of the key resistance movements on both national and pan-Arab level, steadily sinking into a sectarian war against the region's majority.'[17] Nevertheless, the participation of Hezbollah heavily bolsters Assad regime who was getting weaker after some initial defections in the military ranks and the strengthening of the opposition armed forces.

Opposition to the Regime

There are a large number of opposition groups and parties in Syria presently active against the Assad regime. Several armed opposition groups are involved in fighting against the regime's forces. Both political and military opposition to the regime has been fragmented and has lacked cohesion and unity among themselves. Though there are a large number of political groups of different sizes operating from different parts of the country, none of these political entities has become successful to represent the diverse sections of the Syrian society.

Syrian National Council (SNC)

The SNC is one of the first major political bodies to be formed against Assad regime in the aftermath of the beginning of the protests. The SNC is a coalition of groups and individuals, including signatories of the Damascus Declaration (2005), the Syrian Muslim Brotherhood, various Kurdish factions, representatives of the Local Coordination Committees, other political parties or platforms including Damascus Spring and the National Bloc, representatives of the Alawi and Assyrian communities, and some independent figures.[18] Immediately after its formation it emerged as the only political opposition to the Assad regime and therefore many countries around the world started to recognise the SNC as the legitimate representative of the Syrian people.

The SNC sought to secure political support for the Syrian revolution, to promote national unity, to ensure that there is no political vacuum, to develop a roadmap for democratic change in Syria and to deliver the voice of the Syrian revolution and its demands to the international community.[19] Though it had clear objectives, the organisation soon came to face the hurdles for lack of unity among the groups and individuals within the organisation. The trouble with the internal cohesion of the party looked imminent as there were several groups and they represented diverse interests and the leadership did not have any past experience of working together. A common agenda of overthrowing the Assad regime united them together but working to achieve long term goal of establishing a democratic country required unity, commitment and dedication that was found lacking in the organisation. For this reason, there has been frequent changes in the leadership in the SNC which is not a healthy sign for any organisation. The SNC was recognised by a number of countries around the world as the legitimate representative or dialogue partner, prominent among them are the USA, UK, EU, regional countries such as Turkey, Egypt and Arab League.

The Muslim Brotherhood played a major role in the SNC. Muslim Brotherhood's superior organisational structure is one of its strengths in playing an active part in the SNC. Also, the Muslim Brotherhood took the advantage of absence of any other prominent Islamist political organisation active in the country and it became popular among the masses. Their external linkages with the countries like Qatar and Turkey also make them a powerful entity in the country as they receive both ideological and financial support from them. Though it has often been accused of radicalising the protests, the Muslim Brotherhood, nevertheless, has been an important part of the movement against the regime.

National Coalition for Syrian Revolutionary and Opposition Forces

Because of the lack of unity and cohesion it seemed that the SNC was not living up to the expectation of the Syrian people and of the international community. In October 2012, the then US Secretary of State Hillary Clinton stated that "the SNC can no longer be viewed as the visible leader of the opposition", adding that, "it can participate but that opposition must include people from inside Syria and others who have a legitimate voice that needs to be heard."[20] There was apprehension in the US that the SNC is dominated by the Muslim Brotherhood and that the council failed to attract the minorities such as the Kurds, Alawites, Christians, Druze, and so on.[21] Thus, in November 2012 the National Coalition for Syrian Revolutionary and Opposition Forces was formed in Doha which included the SNC and several other political factions and groups. The coalition became a larger umbrella body and is more inclusive in its formation, with the SNC being its largest component. The stated goal of the coalition is to establish a 'democratic, pluralistic Syria based on the rule of law and civil State, where all the Syrians will be equal regardless of their ethnic, religious and sectarian background'.[22] It also declares to uphold the sovereignty, unity and territorial integrity of the country.

The national coalition, since its formation, has received widespread international recognition. The coalition has been recognised by the US, EU, Arab League, GCC, Turkey along with some other countries as the legitimate representative of the Syrian people. The Arab League granted Syria's seat in the organisation to the national coalition and designated it as the main interlocutor with the Arab League. International recognition certainly gives more legitimacy to the coalition to function but its unity is prerequisite as there is always a high probability of internal differences emerging among the members.

The High Negotiation Committee (HNC) of the Opposition Forces

A group of 34 opposition groups backed by Saudi Arabia formed a High Negotiation Committee (HNC) to unify the various opposition groups and to negotiate with the regime in the UN-mediated peace process. The formation of the HNC was decided in December 2015 in a meeting of the opposition groups in Riyadh which was hosted by the Saudi government. But the HNC excluded the Syrian Kurds, Jabhat Al Nusra (now renamed as Jabhat Fateh Al Sham) and some other opposition groups.[23] The HNC has raised objections to the increasing Russian airstrikes in Syria and the regime's airstrikes in inhabited areas. The HNC also appealed the international community to protect the Syrian people from the crimes committed by the Assad regime and its allies and mercenaries. The HNC demanded cessation of violence, humanitarian access and to step up political process in the country. The HNC also appeals that all the UN Security Council resolutions on Syria should be implemented and Assad should leave for any political solution to the crisis.[24] The formation of the HNC prompted different reactions from the external players in Syria. Countries like Saudi Arabia, Qatar, Turkey, and France immediately welcomed the move of the opposition. Russia criticised the formation of the HNC stating that it does not represent all the opposition groups in the country. Similarly the excluded groups such as the Kurds and Al Nusra also condemned the formation of the HNC.

Free Syrian Army (FSA)

The FSA is the military structure under the control of the Syrian national coalition. The FSA was formed in 2011 by the defected officers from the Syrian Army. These are the officers and soldiers who refused to shoot at the protesters and chose to fight with the people against the regime. In December 2012, in a meeting of the military commanders in Turkey, the FSA founded the Supreme Military Council (SMC)[25] – a 30-member body to coordinate operations and strategic planning. The SMC coordinates the military operations undertaken by the FSA. It made efforts to bring all other rebel armed groups under the umbrella of a unified military command so that a robust military front can be formed against the regime. The SMC also tried to create a platform for the development of a countrywide military strategy[26] to fight against the regime's forces. At present, the FSA looks to be the only armed organisation which is united with a command and control structure. It has been financially supported and provided with arms and weapons by countries like the US, Saudi Arabia and Qatar.

Different sources of funding is one of the main challenges facing the FSA. Though all the rebel armed groups have come under a unified FSA, their funding and weapons come from different sources. The FSA or the SMC has little control over the funding of their affiliates. These small groups get funding or weapons by dint of their personal connections or social networks.[27] It has also been reported that Saudi Arabia and Qatar are funding different groups of rebels in the FSA and are trying to exert more influence and impose their ideology. There are also reports of rivalries within the ranks of the FSA which has been a cause of embarrassment for the rebels.[28] Even though the FSA is the main military organisation fighting against the regime, it still lacks the coordination required to undertake large scale operations.

Jihadi Resistance

Jihadis are playing a very crucial role in the opposition to the Assad regime. There are a number of such organisations who are providing strong ideological and military resistance to the regime. They are inspired and driven by their own ideology and objectives. They do not seem to be united because of their differences and prefer to fight independently though they are fighting against a common enemy. Rather, in some cases, they are found to be involved in intermittent clashes among themselves.

The emergence of the ISIS has been one of the most powerful challenges to the Assad regime. The ISIS declared the establishment of a 'Caliphate' in June 2014 and Abu Baqr Al Baghdadi as its Caliph. Since then it has captured a large swath of territories in Iraq and Syria including the border areas and controlling the entry points. By doing so it has challenged the governments of Iraq and Syria and thereby engaging in a long-drawn military conflict with them. It has also challenged the existing regional political order by trying to redraw boundaries in the volatile region. Carving out a space for itself from north-western Iraq and north-eastern Syria, the ISIS occupies a large swath of territory with around eight million inhabitants.[29] It has discarded the Iraq-Syria border drawn by the Sykes-Picot agreement claiming that the agreement is illegitimate as there is no such border existing between the two countries.[30] At the same time, maintaining control over the gained territory has not been easy, as it has to fight the militaries of Iraq, Syria as well as the coalition forces. Though there is no exact information regarding the estimates of the number of fighters involved with the ISIS, initial estimates by the Central Intelligence Agency (CIA) put it around 20,000 to 31,500.[31] In November 2014, the chief of staff to the Iraqi Kurdish leader Masoud Barzani claimed that the total armed men under the caliphate would be around 200,000.[32] Recently, Brett McGurk, Special Presidential Envoy to the Global Coalition to Counter Islamic State of Iraq and Levant (ISIL), stated that at present 30,000 foreign fighters from 100 countries around the world have joined the IS in Iraq and Syria.[33] ISIS has looted weapons from Iraq and is procuring arms from illegal black market as well.[34] It has also confiscated the arms and weapons from the captured territories of Iraq and Syria. The defected military leaders have also managed to bring some weapons along with them.

The Jabhat Fateh Al Sham is another jihadi terrorist organisation which is fighting against the Assad regime. Previously this group was known as Jabhat Al Nusra and was an Al-Qaeda affiliated front.[35] In July 2016, Jabhat Al Nusra severed ties with Al-Qaeda and changed its name. While some scholars believe that this move reflects the evolution of its strategy and a better understanding of Syrian local dynamics,[36] yet others believe that the move is intended to escape from the US list of proscribed terrorist organisation.[37] The group predominantly consists of radical Sunni Islamist jihadists from Syria who are fiercely opposed to the Assad regime. Abu Mohammed Al Golani, the chief of the Al Nusra Front, told *Al Jazeera* in June 2015 that his group has around 30 percent of foreign fighters including Americans, Europeans, Asians, Russians and Chechens.[38] Golani also announced that their main objective in Syria is the overthrow of the Assad regime and defeat of its allies such as the Hezbollah. He also announced that the group would not target the Alawites of Syria or use the Syrian territory as a launchpad to attack the US or the West.[39] In July 2014, after the ISIS declared a caliphate, Al Nusra also declared to establish an Islamic Emirate in Syria intending to draw more support from the masses.[40] The group has a strong presence in the Idlib province. Al Nusra has been designated as a terrorist organisation by the UN Security Council, US, UK, Russia, Canada, Australia, Saudi Arabia, UAE, Iran, Turkey and some other countries as well.

The Salafists are a major force fighting against the Assad regime. There are a number of Salafist groups who are active in the country. In order to give a united combat to the regime, 11 Salafi groups came together to form the Syrian Islamic Front (SIF) in December 2012.[41] Their aim was to establish an Islamic state in Syria, overthrow the Assad regime, called for a Sunni Islamic theocracy in the country and rejected liberal democracy and secularism.[42] In less than a year of its formation, the SIF was disbanded in November 2013. In the same month, seven Salafi rebel armed groups came together to form another coalition called as the 'Islamic Front'.[43] Some of the SIF members also the joined the newly formed Islamic Front. At the time of its formation, the group had around 45,000 fighters in its ranks, and it aims to overthrow the Assad regime and establish an Islamic State in Syria.[44] The Salafi groups are reportedly supported and funded by Saudi Arabia who is worried about the rise of Al-Qaeda in Syria.[45] This provides them a crucial external support to sustain themselves in the war.

Syria and Regional Geopolitics

The developments in Syria has impacted the regional balance of power in the region. As violence and instability has prevailed for a long time, the regional players have come in to exert their influence in the country. An exciting blend of power politics, ideology and sectarianism is at play in Syria. All the major internal players in Syria are supported by some or other external players. The regime has been supported by Iran, Russia and Hezbollah from whom the regime gets arms, funding and the military support on the ground. Similarly, the various rebel groups have also different supporters outside the country. Muslim Brotherhood is alleged to have strong links with Qatar and Turkey. Similarly, Saudi Arabia has been accused of funding and supporting the Salafi groups in Syria. The National Coalition has got wider international recognition and it has been getting support from a large number of countries including the US, Turkey, Saudi Arabia, Qatar among others.

Syria has also further aggravated the relationship between Saudi Arabia and Iran – two major players in the region – with many observers stating that there is a 'proxy war' going on between the two countries. Taking opportunity of the existing situation in Syria, both the countries have been trying increase their own spheres of influence in the country and using the Syrian conflict to maximise their political gains. For Tehran, Syria is a major geopolitical ally in dealing with the United States, Israel, Saudi Arabia and other Gulf Arab states. For Iran, the Lebanese Hezbollah is the most precious asset.[46] On the contrary, for Riyadh, the Assad regime is a hindrance in its interests in Syria and the region as well. There have been no indication from both these countries to mutually discuss the Syrian issue and make attempts to normalise the situation. Rather, the involvement of these powers lead to strengthening of the different groups, leading to further aggravation of the conflict.

Syria is also one of the important reasons for the recent conflict within the Gulf Cooperation Council (GCC). Saudi Arabia, UAE and Bahrain recalled their envoys from Qatar alleging the later's failure to implement an agreement among GCC countries not to interfere in each other's internal affairs.[47] They alleged that Qatar did not respect the agreement it signed which reads, "Anyone threatening the security and stability of the GCC whether as groups or individuals – via direct security work or through political influence, and not to support hostile media."[48] There are political and ideological differences between Saudi Arabia and Qatar. As mentioned earlier, Saudi Arabia supports the Salafists but the Qatar backs the Muslim Brotherhood. There has been an internal tussle between these two countries to increase their power and influence in Syria as both Salafists and the Muslim Brotherhood are actively engaged in opposition to the regime. As the Muslim Brotherhood has played a very important role in the formation of the SNC and has been a dominant force in the national coalition, it has emerged as a major political force in opposition to the Assad regime. For, Saudi Arabia, growing profile of the Muslim Brotherhood in Syria would mean increasing influence of Qatar in Syria and a marginal role for Saudi Arabia in any future political dispensation in the country. Therefore, Saudi Arabia has strengthened the Salafi rebels by uniting them to form the Islamic Front, and later it banned the Muslim Brotherhood as well. Such decisions points to the existence of differences between the two over crucial issues which has been brought to the fore because of the developments in Syria.

GCC States and Syrian Crisis

Ever since the protests started against Assad regime, the Gulf countries have adopted a tough posture by criticising and condemning the reactions of the Syrian government and squarely putting the blame upon it for the unfolding situation. The Gulf monarchies have accused the Assad regime of killings the protesters and violating human rights and have been questioning the regime's legitimacy to continue its rule.

The GCC countries have vociferously demanded regime change in Syria. They have their own reasons to believe that a regime change in Damascus is necessary. The GCC countries do not enjoy a warm relationship with Syria; instead, they see the Assad regime as a strategic ally of Iran. Also, Assad being an Alawite Shia does not get along well with the Sunni rulers of the Gulf. Assad and the Gulf countries have differences of opinions over regional issues such as Iraq, Iran, and Lebanon etc. The proximity of the Gulf countries to the United States and the rivalry between the United States and the Assad regime is another factor that fuels antipathy between the two.

Initially, the Gulf countries appealed to the Syrian government to stop the killings and to adopt adequate reform measures to meet the aspirations of the people. But by the time the Syrian government called for a dialogue and reforms it was clearly too late for the regime to gain support from the people. With the situation going from bad to worse, the Gulf countries exerted more political and diplomatic pressure on Syria and tried to internationalise the issue. They supported the Arab League proposal to establish peace in Syria as well as the mission of the Kofi Annan and his six-point formula which was later adopted by the UN as a road map for bringing peace and stability. The Gulf countries have also backed all the US supported resolutions in the UNSC against the Assad regime. In order to exert further pressure, the Gulf countries decided to recall their ambassadors from Damascus and also expelled Syrian envoys from their countries. They also withdrew their representatives from the Arab League observers' mission in Syria. In November 2012, GCC recognised the opposition National Coalition of the Syrian opposition as the 'legitimate representative' of the Syrian people. Full recognition of the opposition coalition removes all the obstacles in the way of securing arms and weapons for the opposition forces.[49] Recognising the opposition coalition as the legitimate representative of people of Syria would mean delegitimising Assad as the leader of the country.

The Gulf countries' have tried to internationalise the Syrian crisis and such a step is intended to delegitimise and subsequently remove Assad from power. But none of them have any concrete proposal regarding the future roadmap for the country. Despite that, the GCC countries want a Syria without Assad at the top. They would certainly push for a Sunni majority regime which would serve their interest in Syria. At the same time, a weakened Syria minus Assad would lead to a substantial loss of Iranian influence in Syria and in the region as well. Iran has maintained strong ties with the Assad regime and it is seen by the GCC countries as a potential threat to their strategic interests in the region. The Iran-Syria relationship is an important pillar of the 'Shia crescent' threatening traditional Sunni dominance in the region. The Shia resurgence of the last few years has been a major concern for the Sunni regimes in the Gulf.

Two of the GCC countries, Saudi Arabia and Qatar, have openly called for arming the Syrian rebels to fight against the regime's security forces. They believe that all kinds of political and diplomatic initiatives by the regional and world powers have failed, and thus, arming the rebels is the only viable option left with them. Kuwait's parliament has passed a non-binding resolution calling on its government to arm the Syrian rebels. Former Saudi Foreign Minister Prince Saud Al Faisal went to the extent of saying that arming the Syrian opposition is a "duty" as the opposition cannot defend itself in the face of the violent crackdown by the security forces.[50] By supporting the arming of the rebel forces, Saudi Arabia and Qatar seem to be suggesting a Libya-like solution to the Syrian crisis – remove Assad by arming the rebels and install another regime in power. But the Syrian government has, from the beginning, rejected any kind of external invention in its internal affairs. This position was most vocally stated by the Syrian ambassador to the UN, Bashar Jaafari, when he said that, "Syria will not be Libya; Syria will not be Iraq; Syria will not be Somalia; Syria will not be a failing state."[51] Thus, the intensity in the attempts by the Gulf countries to remove Assad and the equally rigorous defiance by the regime have persisted throughout the crisis.

Saudi Arabia has been leading the political and diplomatic offensive against the Assad regime. It has been constantly pressurising the major powers for a regime change in Syria. The Kingdom has also imposed itself as the main regional power supporting the opposition in Syria and has an edge over its smaller neighbours.[52] In a bold move, in October 2013, Saudi Arabia rejected the United Nations Security Council seat as a non-permanent member for which it was elected. It was angered by the repeated vetoes by Russia and China to pass resolutions which would have paved the way for military action against the Assad regime. In an official statement, Saudi Arabia pointed out that no significant action has been taken against Assad even though his regime has used chemical weapons against its own citizens. For Riyadh, this is the 'irrefutable evidence and proof of the inability of the Security Council to carry out its duties and responsibilities'.[53] According to Prince Turki Al Faisal bin Abdul Aziz Al Saud, the former head of Saudi Arabia's general intelligence:

> "There is nothing whimsical about the decision to forego membership in the Security Council. It is a decision based on the ineffectual performance of the body and the necessity of prodding all the members of the UN to enact the reform that will allow for the Palestinian people to shed the inhuman and immoral Israeli occupation of their land; that will rid the Middle East of the lewd display of dancing around nuclear proliferation by the P5+1 and Iran, and removing the Syrian chemical weapons while Israel continues to build up its nuclear, biological and chemical arsenals; and that will bring to a stop the butchering of the Syrian people by a bloodthirsty president who is now enjoying the protection of the Security Council."[54]

For Saudi Arabia, the Assad regime needs to be removed for any credible political transition to take place in Syria. Saudi Foreign Minister Adel Al Jubeir stated that Assad will be removed – if not by a political process then by the use of force against him.[55] Saudi Arabia believes that it is a 'moral duty' to support the opposition in Syria, stating that 'Saudi Arabia will do everything within its capacity' to save the people from the regime.[56] It has been reported that Saudi Arabia has been supplying arms and weapons to the opposition groups.[57] In an interview, Al Jubeir supported the idea of supplying anti-aircraft land to air missile to the rebel groups which he believed will 'change the balance of power on the ground' and also enable the opposition to target the helicopters dropping chemicals and bombing on them.[58]

Like Saudi Arabia, UAE has also been concerned with the developments in Syria. It has called for a political settlement to the conflict and condemned the atrocities of the Assad regime. For UAE, the continuing aggression by the regime against the people has led to radicalisation among the Sunnis in Syria, and that the overthrow of the Assad regime and establishment of a Sunni regime in Syria would end the violence against the people.[59] This was reflected in the speech of UAE Foreign Minister Sheikh Abdullah bin Zayed at the 70th Session of the United Nations General Assembly meeting in October 2015, where he stated that "the Security Council must fulfil its principal mandate and reach a consensus on a settlement for the Syrian crisis to ensure a political transition and the formation of a new government, which encompasses all components of the Syrian society."[60] He also stated that the crisis in Syria has 'led to a political and security vacuum' which has been 'exploited by terrorist organisations, especially ISIS and the Al Nusra Front.'[61] UAE has also taken part in the military operations against the ISIS in Syria.

Qatar has also called for the overthrow of the Assad regime as it believes that the people of Syria have been subjected to violence and atrocities perpetrated by the regime. The absence of the opposition to the regime has created the space for several terrorist groups to operate in Syria. For Qatar, both terrorism and the tyranny of the Assad regime should be brought to an end.[62] Thus, the approach of GCC countries towards the Syrian crisis has shifted from appealing for political reforms to internationalising the issue to arming the regime's opposition. While the advice from the Gulf has fallen on deaf ears in Syria, and political and diplomatic attempts have not yet provided any concrete results, removing the regime by use of force has come to the fore as a doable alternative in the thinking of some of the Gulf monarchies. For them, this is the right opportunity to remove Assad from power and install a friendly regime in Damascus. They have become partially successful in their attempts to internationalise the issue and draw world attention to the wrong doings of the Assad regime. While Assad's removal from power would make it easier for the Gulf countries to intervene in Syria's future political developments and tilt the regional balance of power in their favour, Assad's prolongation in power will continue to pose challenges for them.

Iran and Syrian Crisis

The close relationship between the Assad regime and Iran has been a determining factor in the Syrian crisis. From the beginning of the protests in Syria, Iran has been supporting the Assad regime. Syria became the first case for Iran of supporting a regime during the Arab uprising, who till then was supporting the protesters against the regimes such as in Egypt, Bahrain and Yemen. Iran's ideological position of overthrowing the dictatorial Arab regimes for oppressing people changed when the protests hit Syria. The Iranian government has thrown its weight behind the Assad regime and has provided all kinds of support to save Assad on the face of growing international criticism.

For Iran, Assad has been a trusted ally in the region. The relationship between the two countries gathered momentum in the aftermath of the Islamic Revolution in Iran in 1979. Prior to the Islamic revolution, both countries were antagonistic towards each other as Shah of Iran was an American ally and the socialist Syria in the soviet orbit. Thus, Syria viewed the policies of Shah as an extension of the US policies in the region.[63] The overthrow of the Shah regime by the Islamic revolution in Iran completely changed the situation and Syria became one of the first Arab countries to recognise the new regime in Tehran. The relationship continues to grow stronger since over three decades and has actively shaped the course of regional politics in West Asia. Saddam Hussain's attack on Iran in 1980 and the subsequent Iran-Iraq war that continued till 1988, brought Iran and Syria further closer. Assad condemned the Iraqi aggression on Iran stating that it is a 'wrong war against a wrong enemy at a wrong time.'[64] Syria backed Iran by providing military and diplomatic support. It discreetly supplied Russian made arms and ammunitions to Iran and supplied intelligence on Iraq to Iran.[65] Iran has supported Syria in its war against Israel and its activities in Lebanon. Iranian influence in Lebanon has also been used to the advantage of Syria. Both countries signed a defence cooperation agreement in 2006, further strengthening the relationship.

There are a lot of differences between the two allies in the nature of their regimes and foreign policy priorities. Iran is a conservative

Islamist theocracy with an Ayatollah as the supreme leader of the country. Syria is a Baathist socialist political system with secularism as one of the fundamental principles of the state. In the sphere of foreign policy, Iran's focus is more on the Gulf region whereas Syria lays more attention on the Levant[66] with Israel and Lebanon as its sources of insecurity. But despite such differences both the countries have found common grounds to forge a partnership. Anti-Zionism and anti-imperialist attributes primarily targeting the US are the tendencies which are shared by both the countries in their foreign policies.[67] Both Syria and Iran are designated as the 'state sponsors of terrorism' by the US since 1979 and 1984, respectively.[68] For both, anti-Zionism formed the core of their foreign policy and was an important ideology determining their policies in the region. The blatant anti-American and anti-Israel ideologies that were brought to the fore by the Ayatollah Khomeini in the Islamic revolution in 1979 impeccably matched with the similar line of thinking by Assad. Since then there has been no looking back and the relationship continues on those ideological lines. Both countries have supported the Hamas and the Hezbollah in order to establish a resistance axis against the Israeli aggression in the region. Such commonalities in their foreign policy approach has not only endured their relationship but has also shaped the regional geopolitics in West Asia.

Iran has two broad strategic interests in protecting the Assad regime. Firstly, Iran fears that the Sunnis may capture power in Damascus in the event of Assad being removed from power. This will lead to a dominance of Saudi Arabia and other GCC countries in Syria which would be facilitated by the fact that the majority of the population in Syria are Sunnis.[69] This will change the balance of power in the Levant massively in favour of Saudi Arabia and would be a huge loss for Iran. Secondly, Iran's control over Hezbollah will also be severely affected if it loses Assad. For Iran, Hezbollah is a strategic element in the axis of resistance and loosening of control over Hezbollah will lead to declining Iranian influence in the Levant.

Syria is a strategic partner for Iran working as a bulwark against Saudi Arabia and the GCC countries. On the other hand, Iran is also capitalising upon the antagonistic relationship between Assad regime and the GCC countries. The Assad regime has also a very contentious relationship with the US. This makes Iran and Syria natural allies in the region. Iran remained under sanctions for over a decade which soured its relationship with the US. After the beginning of the crisis in Syria, US and the West has tried to keep Iran away from Syria by accusing it of aggravating the problems in the country. But they have not been successful in containing Iranian activities in Syria. Rather, Iran makes a claim that the West has realised that Iran is a part of the solution in Syria rather than the problem.[70] Despite the best efforts of the US and its Arab Gulf allies to keep Iran away from Syrian affairs, Iran has emerged as a crucial player in the regional geopolitics surrounding Syria. Iran's clout over Assad regime has grown exponentially to such an extent that any regional and international efforts to restore peace and stability in Syria cannot ignore Iran as an important player.

In the complex political spectrum of West Asian region, the sectarian politics has been an important aspect of the alliances and partnership. Both the regimes in Tehran and Damascus are Shias. By forging ties with Syria, Iran has got a platform to spread its Shiite Islamic revolutionary ideology. Alliance with Iran gives Assad regime the required strength and increase its power to deal with its domestic Sunni majority. There are apprehensions of Iran along with Syria and other Shia regimes forming a 'Shia Crescent'. The Sunni dominated regimes such as the GCC states are wary of the Iranian designs in the region and are particular worried about the alliance between Iran and Syria. The Shia religious connection may not have been an important factor in the establishment of the alliance during the early 1980s, but with the changing nature of regional politics, it has emerged as a crucial factor in the current political scenario.

As the protests gathered momentum against Assad, Iran provided technical support and expertise to the security forces to help the Assad regime deal with the protesters. It has also been reported that the specialist personnel and units from the IRGC's elite Qods Force and military advisers from Iran are deployed in Syria to assist the Assad regime defeat the opposition forces.[71] In September 2012, Commander of the IRGC, General Mohammad Ali Jafari, confirmed that several

Qods force are present in Syria though they do not constitute a 'military presence'. General Jafari also stated that Iran is providing 'intellectual and advisory help' to Syrian regime.[72] In June 2015, President Hasan Rouhani, reiterating his country's support for Assad, stated that "the Iranian nation and government will remain at the side of the Syrian nation and government until the end of the road", adding that, "Tehran has not forgotten its moral obligations to Syria and will continue to provide help and support on its own terms to the government and nation of Syria."[73] Iran believes that Assad is not problem in Syria rather the main problem facing the country is terrorism, especially, the ISIS.

Iran urges that the crisis in Syria should be solved by the Syrians themselves. The interference by the regional and extra-regional powers only adds up further complications to the situation. Iran supports a non-military solution to the crisis in Syria and has urged for the resolution of the conflict through political means.[74] Iran emphasises that any change in the regime in Damascus should be done in a democratic manner and people of Syria should be allowed to determine their future.[75] For Iran, negotiations among the Syrian political parties and groups concerned is the best way to reach a political solution in the country and that Syrians are capable of resolving the crisis by themselves.[76]

The survival of the Assad regime is vital for Iranian interests in the region. Any solution to the Syrian crisis which calls for stepping down of Assad will not be acceptable for Iran. Iran calls for a dialogue among the Syrians and for a political solution to the conflict, but at the same time, it has provided funding, weapons and forces to Syria to protect the regime. Assad has come under severe criticism and condemnation from the regional countries many of whom support a regime change in Syria to bring back stability in the country. Besides, the regional organisations such as the GCC, Arab League and the Organisation of Islamic Cooperation (OIC) have also condemned the regime's response towards the opposition and have called for a regime change in Damascus. In such a situation, Iran has been a lone voice supporting the Assad regime. Assad realises that his survival and future depends, to a large extent, on the Iranian political, financial and military backing. The relationship that begun in 1979 has become only further stronger during the Arab Spring protests in Syria where both the countries have realised the importance of their alliance for the regional politics.

UN, US and Russia: Power Politics over Syria

The Syrian crisis has generated heated debates in the UN. Since the aggravation of the conflict in Syria, UN has adopted several measures to cease the violence and to restore peace and stability in the country. As early as on April 27, 2011, the UNSC held a public debate on the developments in Syria. Since then there have been several resolutions tabled and voted upon by the UNSC intended to maintain stability in the country. In October 2011, China and Russia vetoed a draft resolution on Syria. With the situation aggravating, in February 2012, UN appointed former UN Secretary General Kofi Annan as the UN-Arab League Joint Special Envoy for Syria. Kofi Annan proposed a six-point formula for the establishment of peace in Syria as follows:[77]

(1) Commit to work with the Envoy in an inclusive Syrian-led political process to address the legitimate aspirations and concerns of the Syrian people, and, to this end, commit to appoint an empowered interlocutor when invited to do so by the Envoy;

(2) Commit to stop the fighting and achieve urgently an effective United Nations supervised cessation of armed violence in all its forms by all parties to protect civilians and stabilize the country; To this end, the Syrian government should immediately cease troop movements towards, and end the use of heavy weapons in, population centres, and begin pullback of military concentrations in and around population centres;
As these actions are being taken on the ground, the Syrian government should work with the Envoy to bring about a sustained cessation of armed violence in all its forms by all parties with an effective United Nations supervision mechanism.
Similar commitments would be sought by the Envoy from the opposition and all relevant elements to stop the fighting and work with him to bring about a sustained cessation of armed violence in all its forms by all parties with an effective United Nations supervision mechanism;

(3) Ensure timely provision of humanitarian assistance to all areas affected by the fighting, and to this end, as immediate steps, to accept and implement a daily two hour humanitarian pause and

to coordinate exact time and modalities of the daily pause through an efficient mechanism, including at local level;

(4) Intensify the pace and scale of release of arbitrarily detained persons, including especially vulnerable categories of persons, and persons involved in peaceful political activities, provide without delay through appropriate channels a list of all places in which such persons are being detained, immediately begin organising access to such locations and through appropriate channels respond promptly to all written requests for information, access or release regarding such persons;

(5) Ensure freedom of movement throughout the country for journalists and a non-discriminatory visa policy for them;

(6) Respect freedom of association and the right to demonstrate peacefully as legally guaranteed.

The six-point formula was supported by the UNSC as the plan for mediation in Syria. But none of the parties involved in fighting adhered to the plan. As a result, the violence continued unabated resulting in increasing casualties and creating a humanitarian crisis. In June 2012, the UN and the Arab League called an Action Group for Syria meeting which included the Secretary General of the United Nations and Secretary General of the Arab League, the Foreign Ministers of China, France, Russia, United Kingdom, United States, Turkey, Iraq (Chair of the Summit of the Arab League), Kuwait (Chair of the Council of Foreign Ministers of the Arab League) and Qatar (Chair of the Arab Follow-up Committee on Syria of the Arab League) and the European Union High Representative for Foreign and Security Policy.[78] The meeting was held in Geneva and the meeting issued its final communique known as the 'Geneva Communique' on June 30, 2012. It suggested measures to be taken by the parties concerned and urged the parties to implement the six-point plan. Among others measures, the Geneva Communique urged the parties for immediate cessation of violence, allow humanitarian access and agreed on guidelines for a Syrian-led transition in the country.[79] But violence and hostilities continued throughout the country and the Geneva Communique remains one of the reference points for mediation by the UN. Disappointed over the growing militarisation of the conflict and the disagreement among the members of the UNSC, Kofi Annan resigned from his responsibility in August 2012. He stated that the situation on ground continues to aggravate "because of the Syrian government's intransigence, and continuing refusal to implement the six-point plan, and also because of the escalating military campaign of the opposition – all of which is compounded by the disunity of the international community."[80] After the resignation of Annan, Lakhdar Brahimi was appointed as the special envoy to Syria. Brahimi also stepped down as the special envoy in May 2014 and was succeeded by Staffan de Mistura in July 2014.

The reports of the use of chemical weapons by the Assad regime raised serious questions regarding the civil war in Syria. Evidences of use of chemical weapons came out in August 2013 when it was found to have been used in Ghouta. The use of chemical weapons elicited strong international reactions against Assad regime with US President Barack Obama stating it as the 'red line' for the US. Owing to the increasing international pressure, Syria signed the Chemical Weapons Convention in October 2013 and, subsequently, agreed for destruction of all its chemical weapons. The Organisation for the Prohibition of Chemical Weapons (OPCW) played a very important role in supervising the process of destroying the weapons. In October 2013, OPCW found 1,000 metric tons of Category-1 chemical weapons stocks which included most important varieties such as Sarin, 290 tons of Category-2 chemical agents and 1,230 unfilled chemical weapons delivery systems.[81] In the very same month OPCW and the UN established a joint mission to oversee the elimination of all the chemical weapons from Syria. The Joint Mission has been mandated to 'achieve the timely elimination of the Syrian chemical weapons programme in the safest and most secure manner possible'[82] and Sigrid Kaag was appointed as the Special Coordinator for the OPCW-UN Joint Mission. The OPCW has laid out a plan to destroy all the Syria's chemical weapons stock by June 2014. In January 2014, the OPCW reported that the first consignment of priority chemicals were removed from Syria. It also faced difficulty to remove the chemical weapons from the warzones which caused delays for the OPCW. For its sincere efforts towards eliminating chemical weapons in Syria, the OPCW received the 2013 Nobel Prize for peace. The OPCW has also received enormous international support in its efforts to remove all the chemical weapons from Syria.

Apart from the continuing hostilities between the Syrian government and the opposition forces on the ground, the politics over Syria at the high table of the UNSC was also equally controversial. The world powers were sharply divided over the course of action to be taken in Syria to restore order in the country. US and the European countries were in favour of an aggressive approach against the Assad regime and put the blame on the regime for not being able to control the situation. They alleged that the regime itself is indulging in violence against its own population. They also provided financial and military support to the Syrian opposition coalition. In the region, they are supported by their allies such as Saudi Arabia and other GCC countries, Jordan and Egypt. On the other hand, Russia and Iran have supported the Assad regime. Thus, the political and diplomatic lines at the high table on Syria has been clearly demarcated. This is distinctly reflected from the number of resolutions that have been introduced by a group of countries and has been vetoed upon by others, especially Russia and China. On October 4, 2011, a group of countries including France, Germany, Portugal and United Kingdom initiated a draft resolution on Syria which condemned the 'systematic human rights violations and the use of force against civilians by the Syrian authorities' and demanded that the Syrian authorities end violence, stop human rights violations, end use of force against the civilians etc.[83] The draft resolution was vetoed upon by Russia and China. Another draft resolution of similar nature was again initiated on February 4, 2012 by a group of countries including Bahrain, Colombia, Egypt, France, Germany, Jordan, Kuwait, Libya, Morocco, Oman, Portugal, Qatar, Saudi Arabia, Togo, Tunisia, Turkey, UAE, UK and US. This draft again was vetoed upon by Russia and China.

The Assad regime has been a challenge for the US in the region. The Assad regimes of Bashar Al Assad and before him his father Hafez Al Assad's have been blatantly anti-US in their policies. Their close relationship with Iran and Hezbollah has also made the US wary about the Syrian regime.[84] Engaging with Syria has not been a priority for the Obama administration and before that the administration of George W. Bush. The US has chosen to remain engaged with regional powers such as Saudi Arabia, Turkey and Iran, as one scholar opines that US has paid heavy price for not engaging Syria throughout the decades.[85]

Even after the aggravation of the conflict, Obama was not in favour of an American military intervention in Syria. Obama pledged to send troops only if America's 'primary interests' are targeted; which means that he did not view Syria as one of the vital interests.[86] Rather than sending troops Obama preferred a limited involvement in Syria by way of political and military support to the opposition.

US now holds the view that the Assad regime must be removed for any meaningful political process to take place in Syria. The US has also the backing of the Gulf Arab states who strongly demand removal of Assad from power and put the blame on him for the continuing instability in Syria. During the Camp David meeting in May 2015, US and the GCC reiterated their commitment to work together in Syria. Both affirmed that 'Assad had lost all legitimacy and had no role in Syria's future'.[87] They also 'committed to increasing support to the moderate opposition' and at the same time 'to intensify efforts to combat extremist groups in Syria such as ISIS, Al Nusra Front now renamed as Jabhat Fateh Al Sham, and other violent extremist groups.'[88] Only a few months later, the US-GCC Foreign Ministers met in Doha in August 3, 2015. The joint statement issued at the end of the meeting clearly spells out the US-GCC policy approach towards Syria. It stated that:

> "The Ministers reaffirmed their call for a managed political transition in Syria, noting that President Assad has lost all legitimacy. They stressed the necessity of a new Syrian government that reflects the aspirations of the Syrian people and advances national unity, pluralism, and human rights for all Syrian citizens. The Ministers noted the regime has demonstrated neither the will nor the capability to confront terrorist safe havens in Syria. The Ministers also noted the regime's relentless violence against its own people, including the use of barrel bombs and chemical weapons. The Ministers also reaffirmed their ongoing commitment to provide humanitarian assistance to the Syrian people, whose lives have been deeply affected by this crisis, and called upon the regime to permit all needed deliveries of such assistance."[89]

Russian approach runs contrary to that of the US in Syria. From the beginning of the conflict in Syria, Russia has thrown its weight behind the Assad regime. Russia's support for Assad regime has been one of the determining factors in the political and security dynamics of Syria and also of the region. By supporting Assad, Russia has put up a challenge for the US and its Gulf Arab allies in the region who are campaigning for the removal of Assad. Russia's presence in Syria serves as a counter-weight to the American dominance in the region. In the UNSC, Russia has vetoed the attempts by the US and some other European countries trying to condemn the activities of Assad and pass a resolution which could have allowed use of military force against the Assad regime. Rather, Russia has reiterated its continuous support for the regime in future.[90] Russia claims that it is supplying weapons and providing training to the Syrian regime in its fight against the ISIS and other armed opposition groups.[91] On September 30, 2015, Russia conducted its first air strikes against the ISIS in Syria and claimed that the strikes are intended to provide 'air support to the Syrian government forces in their fight against the Islamic State.'[92] Syria is possibly the only foothold in the whole West Asian region which is dominated by the presence of the US. Removal of Assad from power will be a loss for Russian strategic interests in the region. Russia's strategic interest lies in the port of Tartus, which is located in the Mediterranean coast of Syria where Russia maintains a naval facility. This is a crucial strategically located port for Russia for its military support to the Assad regime. Amid the ongoing conflict, Russia is reportedly expanding the Tartus port to handle bigger warships and transport vessels.[93] This shows an unequivocal Russian approach towards Syria: countering the US and its allies from removing Assad and at the same time protecting Assad and maintaining its strategic assets.

Russia is engaging with the like-minded countries of the region in the pretext of fighting the ISIS. In September 2015, to establish a coordinated framework, Iraq, Syria, Iran and Russia formed an intelligence committee in Baghdad to coordinate the actions against the ISIS. The objective of the committee was to share and analyse information as well as to monitor the movements of terrorists.[94] In September 2015, Russia stated that around 2400 Russian nationals have joined the ISIS.[95] The numbers continued to increase and in November 2016, Russian government stated that more than 3200 Russians have left to join the ISIS.[96] Apart from joining the war against the ISIS, Russian involvement also strengthens its strategic position in the region vis-a-vis the US. The alliances such as this alarms the Gulf Arab rulers as well as the US.

The US-Russia duel over the Syria situation has further escalated the intensity of regional politics. Both Putin and Obama strongly disagree over the course of action in Syria. Obama called for removal of Assad as a necessary condition for the establishment of peace in Syria. Russia, on the other hand, believes that the regime of Assad and his military is the only viable force for stability and to fight against the ISIS. Complete divergence in the perceptions of the US and Russia has given a new twist to the situation in West Asia. Russia has built up military bases in Syria which has created concern for the US. Though both US and Russia agree to work for a diplomatic solution to the crisis, their approach in dealing with the problem looks just contrary to each other which will have severe long term impact on the politics and security of the region. Obama and Putin met on the side-lines of the G20 meet in November 15, 2015 in Turkey. Both the leaders agreed on a 'Syrian-led and Syrian-owned political transition'[97] in Syria, but the tactical differences between them over Assad regime seem to continue.

Saudi Arabia, Iran and the ISIS

Ever since the establishment of the Caliphate, the ISIS has been trying not only to consolidate its gains but also spread its activities and influence beyond its borders. Carving out a space for itself from north-western Iraq and north-eastern Syria, the ISIS occupies a large swath of territory with around eight million inhabitants.[98] At the same time, maintaining control over the gained territory has not been easy, as it has to fight the militaries of Iraq, Syria as well as the coalition forces to exist. The ISIS has been trying to portray itself as a legitimate ideological and political entity. More importantly, it has presented itself as the most powerful Sunni entity in the Iraqi-Syrian political and ideological landscape which is otherwise dominated by the Shiite regimes or militias.[99] In Iraq, there are no other strong Sunni groups to challenge the strength of the ISIS. This leaves the ISIS as the most dominant Sunni terrorist group present in the region. If the ISIS manages to stay for a longer period in an advantageous position, it would become easier for it to transform itself into a socially embedded, political, economic and military presence in the region.[100] Ever since the establishment of the Caliphate, the ISIS has suffered a number of military defeats in both Iraq and Syria, but they have not been extinguished from the societal arena where they are involved in radicalisation of youths and drawing them towards their ideology.

The contentious Saudi-Iran relations stand in the way of establishing a joint coalition against the ISIS. Presently, there is no single united front in the region to fight the ISIS. Though the regional countries are contributing militarily in the fight against the ISIS, a united front involving all the countries is lacking. The regional countries very well realise the dangers posed by the ISIS and also understand that the spread of the ISIS should be checked immediately.[101] But the regional political scenario and the relations among themselves and their own varying regional security priorities are the major hindrances to establish cooperation against the ISIS. For instance, Iran has been supporting the regimes of Iraq and Syria to fight against the ISIS. The GCC countries, Jordan, Turkey and Egypt have chosen to join the US-led coalition to defeat the ISIS. A joint political understanding and military cooperation among the regional powers would put up a formidable challenge to the ISIS which is a common enemy for all of them.

With the emergence of the ISIS, the role of Iran has become increasingly significant in the region. The centrality of Iran can be measured from the fact that Iran enjoys significant influence on both Iraq and Syria. Assad is a strategic ally of Iran. Throughout the difficult period of protests and civil war in Syria, Iran has stood by the Assad regime. Iran has provided political support, funding and material support to the Assad regime.[102] Without the Iranian support, it would have been even more difficult for the Assad regime to sustain in the face of internal political opposition, terrorist groups and external pressure. Similarly, the government of Haider Al Abadi in Iraq maintains strong ties with Iran. Ever since the removal of Saddam Husain, Iran-Iraq ties have witnessed a sea change with growing

Iranian influence in Iraq.[103] Bilateral ties in all important fields – political, economic, defence – have been strengthened significantly during last ten years. Iran, for all practical purposes, would like to protect the territorial integrity and sovereignty of Iraq and Syria. Also, it is in the interest of Iran that the regimes of Baghdad and Damascus do not fall in to the hands of ISIS or any other extremist elements. Iran has also made significant economic investments in Iraq as well. Iran is providing military and financial support to both Iraq and Syria in their fight against the ISIS.[104] Because of Iran's troubled relationship with the USA it did not join the global coalition against the ISIS led by the USA,[105] but Iran has committed itself to fight against the ISIS and provide all possible support to Iraqi and Syrian regimes. In tackling the ISIS, Iran has clearly shown that though the objective of both the US and Iran are one and the same, Iran, by going it alone, has asserted its strategic independence, regional leadership and dominance. The fact that Iran has chosen to strike the ISIS without joining hands with the US reflects a deft Iranian strategy in Iraq and Syria. This would mean that Iran would go ahead to strike against the ISIS targets but at the same time would not compromise its strategic independence by calculatingly avoiding any regional military coalition with the US against the ISIS.[106]

The rise of the ISIS and its declaration of a Caliphate came both as a surprise and a challenge for the Kingdom of Saudi Arabia. The growing cadre strength of the ISIS, its control over large parts of Iraq and Syria, running of a parallel economy within Iraq, activities in Syria, and continuous killing of the people have all been causes of concern for the House of Saud. Saudi Arabia has already faced ISIS terror attacks on several occasions. The rise of ISIS poses an ideological challenge for Saudi Arabia as well.[107] Islam has been the most dominant factor in Saudi foreign policy. Saudi Arabia claims itself to be the leader of the Muslim world. The location of the two holy places in its territory has helped Saudi Arabia maintain its dominance and influence in the Islamic world. The ISIS follows the Salafist ideology, which has been supported and promoted by Saudi Arabia. Thus, the announcement of a 'caliphate' by the ISIS challenges Saudi ideological dominance in the region.[108] The ISIS is trying to incite sectarian violence in the region by selectively attacking Shia mosques. The ISIS has launched attacks on Saudi Arabia and alleges that the Saudi regime is corrupt and illegitimate.[109] It calls for overthrow of the Al Saud regime and has proclaimed the goal of capturing the two Holy places of Islam – Mecca and Medina. To incite sectarian violence in the kingdom, the ISIS has targeted Shias in the Eastern Province of Saudi Arabia.[110] ISIS has also undertaken attack of similar nature on Shiite mosques in Kuwait as well.[111] The relationship between Shias and Sunnis in Saudi Arabia has witnessed severe strains in the past. It was further animated during the Arab Spring when people in the Eastern Province, primarily Shias, protested against the regime. ISIS intends to further ignite the sectarian tension in the kingdom by launching attacks on the Shiite mosques and to provoke the Shias against the regime.[112] Further, some Saudi youths being inspired by the ISIS's ideology and joining the organisation undermines the internal security of the kingdom and also challenges the legitimacy of the House of Saud.

In Syria, Saudi Arabia faces the dual challenge of dealing with Bashar Al Assad and the ISIS. It has been at the forefront of opposition to the Assad regime and has severely criticised the atrocities perpetrated by the regime. It has also expressed its discontent over the lack of unified action against Assad by the US and the international community. In Syria, Saudi Arabia has limited influence and that flows from its support for and financing of the Salafists in their fight against the Assad regime. But it has no lever to control the ISIS. Riyadh believes that the removal of Assad from power in Syria would bring the necessary unity and strength to fight against the ISIS in Syria,[113] claiming that removal of Assad is the only possible condition to bring stability in Syria.

The contentious relationship between Saudi Arabia and Iran is a crucial factor hindering establishment of a united military front against the ISIS. In December 2015, Saudi Arabia announced the formation of an Islamic military alliance of 34 Islamic countries, all of them members of the OIC, to fight against the ISIS.[114] This is the latest Saudi initiative to build an alliance against the ISIS by inviting Islamic countries from West Asia, Africa and South Asia.[115] Saudi Arabia has included South Asian countries such as Pakistan, Bangladesh and Maldives in the coalition. The political and military success of the coalition is yet to be seen, but there are two major challenges the coalition would face. Firstly, the formation of the coalition with a deliberate omission of Iran limits its capabilities to achieve its intended objective of defeating the ISIS. The formation of the coalition does not iron out the existing Saudi differences with Iran which is a major factor in building region-wide coalition against the ISIS. Secondly, the members of the coalition are Arab/Islamic countries that are mostly friendly in their approach towards Riyadh. But still, political differences among them also exist which may emerge as a challenge in the way of achieving consensus among them.

Humanitarian Crisis

The continuing fight between the regime's forces and the rebels has created a grave humanitarian crisis in Syria. Though no exact statistics available, more than 400,000 people have been killed and over one million people have been injured since the beginning of the protests in Syria. They include civilians, opposition forces and the military as well. According to the UN Office for the Coordination of Humanitarian Affairs (UNOCHA), as of May 2016, 13.5 million people inside Syria are in need of humanitarian assistance, 4.8 million people have fled the country and another 6.6 million have been internally displaced.[116] UNOCHA figures indicate that 11.5 million Syrians require health care, 13.5 million need protection support and 12.1 million require water and sanitation, while 5.7 million children need education support, including 2.7 million who are out of school in Syria and across the region. About 2.48 million people are food insecure, while more than 1.5 million need shelter and household goods.[117] A report by the UN Secretary General[118] states that with the aggravation of conflict, children have been severely affected in the country. According to the report, in the initial stages of the conflict, violations were committed primarily by the government forces. But increasing number of violations were reported as the conflict intensified and the opposition became more organised and armed. While the government forces have been accused of committing grave sexual violences against children, the opposition forces have been accused of recruitment and use of children in the conflict. According to the report, known perpetrators of grave violations against children include the Syrian Armed Forces; Syrian intelligence forces, Government-associated militias such as the Shabiha; the popular committees (later formalised under the National Defence Forces); Syrian Kurdish armed groups; FSA-affiliated groups; Jabhat Fateh Al Sham; Ahrar Al Sham; ISIS; and other independent or unidentified armed groups.[119]

Conclusion

Syria is going through a very difficult phase of its history. The politics and the society has become highly polarised and disintegrated. Violence and brutality has become an integral part of the approach of both the regime as well as the opposition forces. The international community has expressed its concerns over the death and destruction happening in Syria. The UN and countries around the world have come forward to support the people of the country but it is up to the Syrians themselves to chart out a future path for their country. As it has been reiterated by the UN and many other countries, the future should be led by the Syrians and the international community can only help them achieve their goals.

Both the regime and the opposition remain inflexible in their respective positions. The regime has not hesitated to use force against its own people. The reaction from the armed rebels has also been equally brutal. The present irony is that a political and diplomatic solution looks too remote and the armed violence cannot bring any long term solution to the Syrian conflict. Moreover, the armed opposition lacks unity and cohesion among themselves to put up a united challenge to the Assad regime. None of the parties involved look militarily too powerful to completely defeat and destroy the other; nor are they serious to talk and negotiate. Besides, the opposition is fixated upon removal of Assad and has not been successful to build a future roadmap and a plan of action for the country which would be acceptable for all sections of the society.[120] Though militarily challenged by the opposition, Assad still maintains a strong constituency. The comparative strengths and advantages of both the regime and the opposition has bolstered their respective positions thereby contributing to the prolongation of the civil war in the country.

The involvement of the regional and extra-regional players in the Syria has further aggravated the situation. The government and the opposition forces are being supported by regional and international powers which has strengthened their fighting capability and emboldened their political standing. Thomas Richard Davies notes that in Syria, like in Libya, the involvement of the external players contributed to the initial non-violent protests being transformed to large scale violence as these powers advocated use of force and provided resources, weapons and technology to the groups.[121] The fighting in Syria has taken a sectarian colour with the backing of the regional powers particularly, Saudi Arabia and Iran. Their support for the opposition coalition and the regime respectively has provided them further political, economic and military strength to continue their fight. This further perpetuates and aggravates the sectarian tensions in the country. Amid the crisis, Syria has turned out to be a strategically important country for both the players. Despite the political and strategical calculations by Saudi Arabia and Iran, there have been some sincere efforts by the UN attempting to bring the government and the opposition forces to the negotiating table. While the negotiations continue, the future of Syria remain uncertain.

END NOTES

1. "Syria unrest: Who are the Shabiha?", *BBC News*, May 29, 2012, at http://www.bbc.com/news/world-middle-east-14482968.
2. "Syria's paramilitary gangs a law unto themselves", *Reuters*, July 2, 2012, at http://www.reuters.com/article/2012/07/02/us-syria-crisis-shabbiha-idUSBRE8610N620120702.
3. "Syria's Alawite Force Turned Tide for Assad", *Wall Street Journal*, August 26, 2013, at http://www.wsj.com/articles/SB10001424127887323997004578639903412487708.
4. "Insight: Battered by war, Syrian army creates its own replacement", *Reuters*, April 21, 2013, at http://www.reuters.com/article/us-syria-crisis-paramilitary-insight-idUSBRE93K02R20130421.
5. See Aron Lund, "Who Are the Pro-Assad Militias?", Carnegie Endowment for International Peace, March 2, 2015 at http://carnegieendowment.org/syriaincrisis/?fa=59215.
6. Ibid.
7. "Syria: Pro-Government Paramilitary Forces", The Carter Centre, November 5, 2013, at https://www.cartercenter.org/resources/pdfs/peace/conflict_resolution/syria-conflict/Pro-GovernmentParamilitaryForces.pdf.

8. Bassam Haddad, "Syria's Stalemate: The Limits of Regime Resilience", *Middle East Policy*, 19 (1), Spring 2012, p. 88.
9. Yaakov Amidror, "The Hizballah-Syria-Iran Triangle", *Middle Review of International Affairs*, 11 (1), March 2007, p. 4.
10. "Hezbollah is helping Assad fight Syria uprising, says Hassan Nasrallah", *The Guardian*, April 30, 2014, at http://www.theguardian.com/world/2013/apr/30/hezbollah-syria-uprising-nasrallah.
11. "Nasrallah: Hezbollah in Syria for long haul", *Al Jazeera*, November 15, 2013, available at http://www.aljazeera.com/news/middleeast/2013/11/nasrallah-hezbollah-syria-long-haul-2013111414617430132.html.
12. Ali Alfoneh, "Hezbollah Fatalities in the Syrian War", The Washington Institute, Policy Watch 2566, at http://www.washingtoninstitute.org/policy-analysis/view/hezbollah-fatalities-in-the-syrian-war.
13. Chafic Choucair, "Hezbollah in Syria: Gains, Losses and Changes", Al Jazeera Centre for Studies, June 1, 2016, at http://studies.aljazeera.net/mritems/Documents/2016/6/1/694b753fbf784a838e3c81673f2996ce_100.pdf.
14. For the geographical expansion of Hezbollah in Syria see Alex Rowell, "Mapping Hezbollah's Syria war since 2011", August 8, 2015, at https://now.mmedia.me/lb/en/reportsfeatures/565725-mapping-hezbollahs-syria-war-since-2011.
15. "Syria: Hezbollah training Alawite elite force", *Asharq Al Awsat*, September 30, 2012, at http://english.aawsat.com/2012/09/article55240427/syria-hezbollah-training-alawite-elite-force.
16. "Hezbollah leader promises to continue fighting in Syria", *Middle East Eye*, March 22, 2016, at http://www.middleeasteye.net/news/hezbollah-leader-promises-continue-fighting-syria-122175648.
17. Chafic Choucair, "Hezbollah in Syria: Gains, Losses and Changes", n.13.
18. "The Syrian National Council", Carnegie Middle East Centre, September 25, 2013, available at http://carnegie-mec.org/publications/?fa=48334.
19. See their website http://www.syriancouncil.org/en/objectives.html.
20. "As Fighting Rages, Clinton Seeks New Syrian Opposition", *The New York Times*, October 31, 2012, available at http://www.nytimes.com/2012/11/01/world/middleeast/syrian-air-raids-increase-as-battle-for-strategic-areas-intensifies-rebels-say.html?_r=0.
21. Ibid.
22. "Declaration by the national coalition for Syrian revolutionary and opposition forces", available at http://www.etilaf.org/en/coalition-documents/declaration-by-the-national-coalition-for-syrian-revolutionary-and-opposition-forces.html.
23. For the details of the composition of the High Negotiation Committee see Aron Lund, "Syria's Opposition Conferences: Results and Expectations", Carnegie Endowment for International Peace, December 11, 2015, at http://carnegieendowment.org/syriaincrisis/?fa=62263.
24. "HNC Insists on Need to Enforce UN Resolutions & Assad's Departure", The National Coalition for Syrian Revolutionary and Opposition Forces June 3, 2016, at http://en.etilaf.org/all-news/news/hnc-insists-on-need-to-enforce-un-resolutions-assad-s-departure.html.

25. "Rebel Groups in Syria Make Framework for Military", *New York Times*, December 7, 2012, at http://www.nytimes.com/2012/12/08/world/middleeast/rebel-groups-in-syria-make-framework-for-military.html?_r=0, accessed on February 2, 2014.
26. Elizabeth O'Bagy, "The free Syrian Army", Middle East Security Report - 9, Institute for the Study of War, March 2013, available at http://www.understandingwar.org/sites/default/files/The-Free-Syrian-Army-24MAR.pdf, accessed on January 12, 2014.
27. "Who is the Free Syrian Army?", *France 24*, August 10, 2012, available at http://observers.france24.com/content/20120810-syria-free-syrian-army-structure-funding-ideology-methods-fight-against-assad-regime.
28. "Fresh splits within Syria rebel ranks", *Al Jazeera*, August 17, 2013, at http://www.aljazeera.com/news/middleeast/2013/08/20138177464396633.html.
29. "Life under the ISIS caliphate", *The Week*, August 22, 2015, at http://theweek.com/articles/572910/life-under-isis-caliphate.
30. Meghan Tinsley, "ISIS's aversion to Sykes-Picot tells us much about the group's future plans", Muftah.org, April 23, 2015, at http://muftah.org/the-sykes-picot-agreement-isis/#.Vhk4VXnotjo.
31. "ISIS can 'muster' between 20,000 and 31,500 fighters, CIA says", *CNN*, September 12, 2014, at http://edition.cnn.com/2014/09/11/world/meast/isis-syria-iraq/.
32. "War with Isis: Islamic militants have army of 200,000; claims senior Kurdish leader", *The Independent*, November 14, 2014, at http://www.independent.co.uk/news/world/middle-east/war-with-isis-islamic-militants-have-army-of-200000-claims-kurdish-leader-9863418.html?printService=print.
33. Press briefing, "Coalition Efforts against ISIL", by Brett McGurk, Special Presidential Envoy to the Global Coalition to Counter ISIL, November 20, 2015, US Department of State, Washington, D.C., at http://www.state.gov/r/pa/prs/ps/2015/11/249856.htm.
34. "Taking stock: The arming of Islamic State", Amnesty International, December 7, 2015, at https://www.amnesty.org/en/documents/mde14/2812/2015/en/
35. For a detailed discussion see Seth G. Jones, "Syria's Growing Jihad", *Survival: Global Politics and Strategy*, 55(4), 2013, pp. 53-72.
36. Mona Alami, "Jabhat al-Nusra's rebranding is more than simple name change", *Al Monitor*, August 5, 2016, at http://www.al-monitor.com/pulse/originals/2016/08/jabhat-al-nusra-sever-al-qaeda-focus-local-syria.html.
37. Martin Chulov, "Al-Nusra Front cuts ties with al-Qaida and renames itself", *The Guardian*, July 28, 2016, at https://www.theguardian.com/world/2016/jul/28/al-qaida-syria-nusra-split-terror-network.
38. "Nusra leader: No end to conflict with ISIL in Syria", *Al Jazeera*, June 4, 2015, at http://www.aljazeera.com/news/2015/06/nusra-leader-conflict-isil-syria-150604021024858.html.
39. "Nusra leader: Our mission is to defeat Syrian regime", *Al Jazeera*, May 28, 2015, at http://www.aljazeera.com/news/2015/05/nusra-front-golani-assad-syria-hezbollah-isil-150528044857528.html.
40. Hassan Hassan, "Al Nusra declares an 'Islamic emirate', but is it significant?" *The National*, July 15, 2014, at http://www.thenational.ae/opinion/comment/al-nusra-declares-an-islamic-emirate-but-is-it-significant#full.

41. The 11 groups of the SIF included Kataeb Ahrar al-Sham, Liwa al-Haqq, Harakat al-Fajr al-Islamiya, Jamaat Al Taliaa Al Islamiya, Kataeb Ansar Al Sham, Katibat Moussaab bin Omeir, Jaish Al Tawhid, Kataeb Suqour Al Islam, Kataeb Al Iman Al Muqatila, Saraya Al Mahamm Al Khassa and Katibat Hamza bin Abdelmuttaleb.
42. For an analysis of the Syrian Islamic Front in Syria see Aron Lund, "Syria's Salafi insurgents: The rise of the Syrian Islamic Front", UI Occasional papers-17, The Swedish Institute of International Affairs, March 2013, at http://www.ui.se/eng/upl/files/86861.pdf.
43. The Islamic Front includes seven groups namely, Liwa Al Tawhid, Ahrar Al Sham, Soqour Al Sham, the Al Haq Brigades, Ansar Al Sham, Army of Islam, and the Kurdish Islamic Front.
44. Lisa Lundquist, "Formation of Islamic Front in Syria benefits jihadist groups", *The Long War Journal*, November 23, 2013, at http://www.longwarjournal.org/archives/2013/11/yesterday_a_new_isla.php.
45. "Saudi Arabia boosts Salafist rivals to Al-Qaeda in Syria", *Reuters*, October 1, 2013, at http://www.reuters.com/article/us-syria-crisis-jihadists-insight-idUSBRE9900RO20131001.
46. Mohsen Milani, "Why Tehran Won't Abandon Assad(ism)", *The Washington Quarterly*, 36 (4), 2013, p. 88.
47. "KSA, Bahrain, UAE recall ambassadors from Qatar", *Arab News*, March 5, 2014, at http://www.arabnews.com/news/535101.
48. Ibid.
49. "GCC recognises new Syrian opposition bloc", *Al Jazeera*, November 13, 2012, at http://www.aljazeera.com/news/middleeast/2012/11/20121112175539534504.html.
50. "Saudi foreign minister says supporting Syrian opposition is a 'duty'", *Al Arabiya*, March 31, 2012, at https://english.alarabiya.net/articles/2012/03/31/204429.html.
51. "Syrian Rebels Make Inroads with Help of Armed Fighters", *New York Times*, January 27, 2012, at http://www.nytimes.com/2012/01/28/world/middleeast/violence-rises-sharply-in-syria-flustering-arab-league-monitors.html?_r=0.
52. "Saudi edges Qatar to control Syrian rebel support", *Reuters*, May 31, 2013, at http://www.reuters.com/article/us-syria-crisis-saudi-insight-idUSBRE94U0ZV20130531.
53. "Foreign Ministry Makes Statement on Saudi Arabia's Apology for Not Accepting Security Council Membership", *Saudi Press Agency*, October 18, 2013, at http://www.spa.gov.sa/viewstory.php?newsid=1158978.
54. Turki Al Faisal bin Abdul Aziz Al Saud, "Saudi Arabia's Foreign Policy", *Middle East Policy*, 20 (4), Winter 2013, p. 44.
55. "Force Assad out: Kingdom", *Arab News*, February 14, 2016, at http://www.arabnews.com/saudi-arabia/news/880396.
56. "Saudi Arabia, US put Syria, Iran on notice", *Arab News*, March 5, 2013, at http://www.arabnews.com/saudi-arabia/saudi-arabia-us-put-syria-iran-notice.
57. "New Saudi-supplied missiles boost rebels in south Syria", *Reuters*, August 15, 2013, at http://www.reuters.com/article/us-syria-crisis-arms-idUSBRE97E0QH20130815.

58. See the interview of Adel Al Jubeir with *Spiegel*, February 19, 2016, at http://www.spiegel.de/international/world/interview-with-saudi-foreign-minister-adel-al-jubeir-on-syrian-war-a-1078337.html.
59. Alissa Fromkin, "UAE Foreign Policy in Iraq & Syria", *International Affairs Review*, March 5, 2015, at http://www.iar-gwu.org/content/part-three-uae-foreign-policy-iraq-syria.
60. "Abdullah bin Zayed: United Arab Emirates stands firm with the Kingdom of Arabia against any Iranian attempts to interfere in the internal affairs of the Arab States", *Emirates News Agency*, October 3, 2015, at https://www.wam.ae/en/news/emirates/1395286245103.html.
61. See the full text of the speech of the UAE Foreign Minister Sheikh Abdulla Bin Zayed Al Nahyan, "The General Debate of the 70th Session of the United Nations General Assembly", October 2, 2015, at https://www.un.int/uae/statements_speeches/general-debate-70th-session-united-nations-general-assembly-1.
62. See interview of Qatari Foreign Minister Khalid Al-Attiyah with *The New Statesman*, September 29, 2015, at http://www.newstatesman.com/world/middle-east/2015/09/exclusive-interview-qatari-foreign-minister-syria-and-refugee-crisis.
63. For a detailed history and evolution of Iran-Syria relationship see Lorenzo Trombetta, "Syria and Iran in a Middle East in Transition", in Michel Korinman and John Laughland (eds.), *Shia power: next target Iran?*, Vallentine Mitchell Academic, London, 2007, pp. 313-322.
64. Patrick Seale and Maureen McConville, *Asad of Syria: The Struggle for the Middle East*, I.B. Tauris, London, 1988, p. 357.
65. Dilip Hiro, *The Longest War: The Iran-Iraq Military Conflict*, Grafton Books, London, 1989, p. 80.
66. Jubin M. Goodarzi, "Syria and Iran: Alliance Cooperation in a Changing Regional Environment", *Ortadoðu Etütleri*, 4 (2), January 2013, pp.31-54.
67. Nadia von Maltzahn, *The Syria-Iran Axis: Cultural Diplomacy and International Relations in the Middle East*, I.B. Tauris, London, 2013, p. 28.
68. "State Sponsors of Terrorism Overview", US Department of State, at http://www.state.gov/j/ct/rls/crt/2014/239410.htm.
69. Karim Sadjadpour, "Iran's Unwavering Support to Assad's Syria", *Yale Global Online*, August 30, 2013, at http://yaleglobal.yale.edu/content/iran%E2%80%99s-unwavering-support-assad%E2%80%99s-syria.
70. Mostafa Zahrani, "The Role of Iran in Search for Regional Stability", IPIS Commentary, June 2014, Institute for Political and International Studies, at http://ipis.ir/uploads/commentary_zahrani_3.pdf.
71. "Iran says 13 IRGC forces killed in Syria", *PressTV*, May 7, 2016, at http://www.presstv.ir/Detail/2016/05/07/464455/Iran-Syria-IRGC-Khan-Tuman-Aleppo.
72. "Iran confirms it has forces in Syria and will take military action if pushed", *The Guardian*, September 16, 2012, at http://www.theguardian.com/world/2012/sep/16/iran-middleeast.
73. "Iran's Rouhani vows to back Syria 'until the end of the road'", *Reuters*, June 2, 2015, at http://www.reuters.com/article/us-mideast-crisis-syria-iran-idUSKBN0OI0UF20150602.

74. "President Rohani Confers with UN Special Representative for Syria", Ministry of Foreign Affairs, Iran, October 27, 2013, at http://en.mfa.ir/index.aspx?siteid=3&pageid=2014&newsview=16272&pro=nobak.
75. "Deputy Foreign Minister Advises Democratic Means to Resolve Syrian Crisis", Ministry of Foreign Affairs, Iran, July 22, 2015, at http://en.mfa.ir/index.aspx?siteid=3&pageid=2023&newsview=350372&pro=nobak.
76. "Foreign Minister: Syria Capable of Resolving Crisis", Ministry of Foreign Affairs, Iran, June 1, 2014, at http://en.mfa.ir/index.aspx?siteid=3& pageid=2029&newsview=292692&pro=nobak.
77. "Six-Point Proposal of the Joint Special Envoy of the United Nations and the League of Arab States", United Nations, April 14, 2012, at http://www.un.org/en/peacekeeping/documents/six_point_proposal.pdf.
78. "Action Group for Syria Final Communiqué", United Nations, June 30, 2012, at http://www.un.org/News/dh/infocus/Syria/FinalCommuniqueActionGroupforSyria.pdf.
79. Ibid.
80. "Opening remarks by Kofi Annan, Joint Special Envoy for Syria, at press conference – Geneva", UN News Centre, August 2, 2012, at http://www.un.org/apps/news/infocus/Syria/press.asp?NewsID=1245&sID=41.
81. "Syria: Inspectors find 1,300 tons of chemical weapons", *The Telegraph*, October 29, 2013, at http://www.telegraph.co.uk/news/worldnews/middleeast/syria/10411375/Syria-inspectors-find-1300-tons-of-chemical-weapons.html.
82. See the "Joint Statement from the Organisation for the Prohibition of Chemical Weapons (OPCW) and the United Nations (UN)", October 16, 2013, at http://www.opcw.org/news/article/joint-statement-from-the-organisation-for-the-prohibition-of-chemical-weapons-opcw-and-the-united/.
83. See the full text of the draft "France, Germany, Portugal and United Kingdom of Great Britain and Northern Ireland: draft resolution", United Nations Security Council, October 4, 2011, at http://www.un.org/en/ga/search/view_doc.asp?symbol=S/2011/612.
84. Stephen Zunes, "U.S. Policy towards Syria and the Triumph of Neoconservativism", *Middle East Policy*, 11 (1), 2004, pp. 52-69.; also see Mir H. Sadat and Daniel B. Jones, "U.S. Foreign Policy toward Syria: Balancing Ideology and National Interests", *Middle East Policy*, 16 (2), Summer 2009.
85. Joshua Landis, "The U.S.-Syria Relationship: A Few Questions", *Middle East Policy*, 17 (3), Fall 2010, p. 64.
86. Fawaz A. Gerges, "The Obama approach to the Middle East: The end of America's moment?", *International Affairs*, 89 (2), 2013, p. 309.
87. "Annex to U.S.-Gulf Cooperation Council Camp David Joint Statement", The White House, May 14, 2015, at https://www.whitehouse.gov/the-press-office/2015/05/14/annex-us-gulf-cooperation-council-camp-david-joint-statement.
88. Ibid.
89. "Joint Statement of the U.S.-GCC Foreign Ministers Meeting", US Department of State, August 3, 2015, at http://www.state.gov/r/pa/prs/ps/2015/08/245619.htm.
90. "Putin reiterates support for Syria's Assad", *Al Jazeera*, June 18, 2015, at http://www.aljazeera.com/news/2015/06/putin-reiterates-support-syria-assad-150619161453457.html.

91. "Russia supplies Syria with weapons, to put squeeze on US over Assad", *Pravda*, August 21, 2015, at http://english.pravda.ru/news/world/21-08-2015/131701-syria-0/.
92. "Russia Approves Use of Armed Forces in Syria", *Sputnik News*, September 30, 2015, at http://sputniknews.com/russia/20150930/1027761651/russian-armed-forces-abroad.html.
93. "Why Russia Is Expanding Its Naval Base in Syria", *Moscow Times*, September 21, 2015, at http://www.themoscowtimes.com/business/article/why-russia-is-expanding-its-syrian-naval-base/531986.html.
94. "Iraq steps up anti-Daesh coordination with Iran, Syria, Russia", *Khaleej Times*, September 27, 2015, at http://www.khaleejtimes.com/region/mena/iraq-steps-up-anti-daesh-coordination-with-iran-syria-russia.
95. "Some 2,400 Russians fighting for ISIL – Russian FSB", *News.Az*, September 18, 2015, at http://www.news.az/articles/russia/101259.
96. "3200 Russians joined ISIS since start of conflict: government", *Iraqi News*, November 21, 2016 at http://www.iraqinews.com/iraq-war/3200-russians-joined-isis-since-start-conflict-government/.
97. "Obama, Putin agree on need for political transition, ceasefire in Syria: U.S. official", *Reuters*, November 15, 2015, at http://www.reuters.com/article/us-g20-turkey-syria-idUSKCN0T40XH20151115.
98. "Life under the ISIS caliphate", *The Week*, August 22, 2015, at http://theweek.com/articles/572910/life-under-isis-caliphate.
99. James Fromson and Steven Simon, "ISIS: The Dubious Paradise of Apocalypse Now", *Survival*, 57 (3), June-July 2015, p. 40.
100. Ahmed S. Hashim, "The Islamic State: From al-Qaeda Affiliate to Caliphate", *Middle East Policy*, 21 (4), 2014, p. 80.
101. "Gulf states condemn Islamic State jihadists", *Arab News*, August 30, 2014, at http://www.arabnews.com/featured/news/622676. and; see the statement by Iranian Supreme Leader Ayatollah Seyyed Ali Khamenei, after meeting Iraqi President Fuad Masum in Tehran on May 14, 2015, at http://www.leader.ir/langs/en/index.php?p=contentShow&id=13186.
102. W. Andrew Terrill, "Iran's Strategy for Saving Assad", *Middle East Journal*, 69 (2), 2015, pp. 223-236.
103. Kayhan Barzegar, "Iran's Foreign Policy Strategy after Saddam", *The Washington Quarterly*, 33 (1), 2010, pp. 173-189,
104. "Commander: Iran to Supply Iraq, Syria with Further Military Aid", *Fars News*, September 22, 2015, at http://english.farsnews.com/newstext.aspx?nn=13940631000889, also; Will Fulton, Joseph Holliday, & Sam Wyer, "Iranian strategy in Syria", Institute for the Study of War, May 2013, at http://www.understandingwar.org/sites/default/files/IranianStrategyinSyria-1MAY.pdf.
105. "President Blasts 'Ridiculous' U.S. Coalition", *Kayhan*, September 19, 2014, at http://kayhan.ir/en/news/5283/president-blasts-%E2%80%98ridiculous%E2%80%99-us-coalition.
106. Prasanta Kumar Pradhan, "The Kingdom and the Caliphate: Saudi Arabia's approach towards the Islamic State", IDSA Issue Brief, February 3, 2015, at http://www.idsa.in/issuebrief/SaudiArabiaandIslamicState_pkpradhan_020215.

107. James M. Dorsey, "Islamic State: Ideological Challenge to Saudi Arabia", RSIS commentary no. 173, September 3, 2014, at https://www.rsis.edu.sg/wp-content/uploads/2014/09/CO14173.pdf.
108. Madawi Al Rasheed, "Saudi Arabia forced to rethink ideology in fight against IS", *Al Monitor*, December 2, 2014 at http://www.al-monitor.com/pulse/originals/2014/12/saudi-kingdom-versus-caliphate.html.
109. "Islamic State claims 2nd suicide bombing at Saudi mosque", *Chicago Tribune*, May 29, 2015, at http://www.chicagotribune.com/news/nationworld/ct-islamic-state-suicide-bombing-saudi-arabia-mosque-20150529-story.html.
110. "Five killed in Saudi Arabia shooting", *Al Jazeera*, November 4, 2014, http://www.aljazeera.com/news/middleeast/2014/11/five-killed-saudi-arabia-shooting-201411415719478695.html.
111. "IS suicide bomber kills 25 at Kuwait Shia mosque", *Gulf Times*, June 26, 2015, at http://www.gulf-times.com/region/216/details/444747/is-suicide-bomber-kills-25-at-kuwait-shia-mosque.
112. Bilal Y. Saab, "Can the House of Saud survive ISIS?", *Foreign Affairs*, June 11, 2015, at https://www.foreignaffairs.com/articles/2015-06-11/can-house-saud-survive-isis.
113. Nawaf Obaid and Saud Al Sarhan, "A Saudi view on the Islamic State," European Council on Foreign Relations, October 2, 2014, at http://www.ecfr.eu/article/commentary_saudi_arabia331.
114. "Led by KSA, 34-nation alliance to wipe out terror", *Arab News*, December 15, 2015, at http://www.arabnews.com/news/850596.
115. The members of the coalition are Bahrain, Bangladesh, Benin, Chad, Comoros, Djibouti, Egypt, Gabon, Guinea, Ivory Coast, Jordan, Kuwait, Lebanon, Libya, Malaysia, Maldives, Mali, Mauritania, Morocco, Niger, Nigeria, Pakistan, Palestine, Qatar, Saudi Arabia, Senegal, Sierra Leone, Somalia, Sudan, Togo, Tunisia, Turkey, UAE and Yemen.
116. The UN Office for the Coordination of Humanitarian Affairs (UNOCHA), available at http://www.unocha.org/syria.
117. "Syria Crisis: Regional Overview", The UN Office for the Coordination of Humanitarian Affairs (UNOCHA), available at http://www.unocha.org/syrian-arab-republic/syria-country-profile/about-crisis.
118. United Nations Security Council, "Report of the Secretary-General on children and armed conflict in the Syrian Arab Republic", January 27, 2014, available at http://daccess-dds-ny.un.org/doc/UNDOC/GEN/N13/627/07/PDF/N1362707.pdf?OpenElement.
119. Ibid.
120. Fred H. Lawson, "Syria's mutating civil war and its impact on Turkey, Iraq and Iran", *International Affairs*, 90 (6), 2014, p. 1351.
121. Thomas Richard Davies, "The failure of strategic nonviolent action in Bahrain, Egypt, Libya and Syria: 'Political ju-jitsu' in reverse", *Global Change, Peace & Security*, 26 (3), 2014, p. 303.

5

Sectarianism in West Asia: Key Trends

The unrelenting sectarian conflicts continuing in different parts of West Asia, especially in countries like Yemen, Syria and Bahrain have become an overriding phenomena in the region's political and security landscape. The involvement of the people, regimes, militaries, terrorist groups, regional powers, and extra-regional powers in the deadly conflicts has resulted in killing, internal displacement, forced migration, political instability and economic hardship. The sectarian divisions in these societies have become more vociferous and in times of crisis the sectarian identity has overtaken the national identities of the people. The Arab Spring facilitated and created conditions where the sectarian divide became more pronounced and politicised.

Initially, the protests against the regimes were usually peaceful and non-violent. The protesters demanded political and economic reforms, social equality, non-discrimination, employment, human rights, end to corruption, etc. But as the protests were taking place simultaneously in a number of countries, as a result of the domino effect, they gathered momentum very quickly. The protesters used the social media, mobile phones and internet to spread their message. The rapid spread of the popular protests unnerved the rulers and made them wary about their regime security. They then resorted to the use of force to deal with the protesters. In places such as Egypt, Syria, Bahrain and Libya the authorities used disproportionate military force on the protesters. Tanks and heavy weapons were used against the protesters in Egypt, Syria, Yemen and Bahrain. Continuous deterioration of the situation gradually weakened the state and its law enforcement system. Daniel Byman, giving the examples of Iraq and Lebanon, states that when order breaks down, 'communities look inwards' for protection.[1] With their own government using force against them, the tribal, communitarian and sectarian affiliations and identities have become stronger. People began looking up to their social and religious roots for protection against the regimes' atrocities, thus making them take up arms. Gradually, the nonviolent protests transformed itself into violent clashes between protesters and regimes' forces, leading to further chaos and deterioration of the situation.

Sectarian Politics: Key Trends

Deteriorating Saudi-Iran Relationship

The tense Saudi-Iran relationship has further deteriorated as a result of the Arab Spring. Their race for regional supremacy, ideological conflict, rival strategic interests etc. has deepened. Iranian scholars Mahdi Mohammad Nia and Abdolmajid Seifi note that 'identity' plays an important role in the foreign policy behaviours of both Saudi Arabia and Iran. In Saudi Arabia, elements like Arabism, Wahhabism, the kingdom system and huge oil resources are reflected in its foreign policy behaviour in the region. For Iran, political Islam, Persian nationalism, anti-hegemonism and justice-seeking policy etc. are determinants of its foreign policy behaviour in the region.[2] The Arab Spring created a conducive environment, as a result of which the possibilities of accommodation became thinner as each intended to maximise its gains out of an atmosphere of continuing uncertainty. The stakes and involvement of Saudi Arabia and Iran in the present conflicts such as Bahrain, Syria and Yemen show that their rivalry will continue in the near future. This has impacted the regional politics[3] as both the countries view regional politics 'in an ideological zero-sum term'.[4] In the process both countries have bolstered their image of being sectarian powers in the region.

Internal Discrimination by the Regimes

The sectarian politics and the related violence in the region have their roots in the discriminatory policies adopted by the regimes, which have often discriminated against the religious minorities in their countries. Long-term discrimination has fuelled dissent among some sections of society. There have been longstanding complaints by the Shias in the Arab Gulf countries regarding the political, economic and religious discrimination at the hands of the regime. Saudi Shias, who constitute around 10-15 percent of the population, have appealed to the King repeatedly in the past demanding equal rights, reforms, religious equality, employment opportunities, etc., but in vain. In Bahrain, the Shia majority has been complaining of political, economic and religious discrimination by the Sunni-minority rulers. The Shias of Bahrain are not represented in the higher echelons of politics, bureaucracy, military or security services. Bahrain's Khalifa family looks at the Shias as being loyal towards Iran, and thus untrustworthy. There have been allegations of torture, unlawful detention and killings of the Shias at the hands of the regime.

Saddam Hussein's regime was highly discriminatory against the Shias in Iraq. He was also brutal towards the Kurds, who demanded autonomy for Kurdistan. In the post-Saddam era, the Sunnis have been complaining of discriminatory policies adopted by the Shia-dominated government in Baghdad. Many Sunnis have turned to extremism and terrorism to fight the regime. In Syria, the Bashar Al Assad regime has discriminated against the Sunnis, Kurds and Christians.

In Yemen, the regime of Ali Abdullah Saleh faced many internal dissensions from the Houthis as well as from the Southerners. The Houthis, who belong to the Zaidi Shia sect, are gravely dissatisfied with the regime's policies. They have accused the regime of widespread corruption and socio-economic negligence of the Shias. They are also infuriated at the growing influence of Sunni Wahhabism in the country and the country's alliance with the USA. They took to arms and started an armed rebellion from Saada province. The Southerners in Yemen have also complained about discrimination by the government. Southern Yemen has remained relatively poor compared to the north, whereas much of the country's natural resources are located in the south. Political leaders from the north have also dominated political decision-making in the country.

Use of the Sectarian Card for Foreign Policy Objectives

The states in the region have also played the sectarian card for their foreign policy objectives to insulate themselves from the protesters, sowing division in their societies as a matter of policy. Such actions by the regimes have provoked the opposition to get united on sectarian lines against the regime. Bahrain's Khalifa regime gained the support of the Sunni regimes and acted against the protesters. The regime also played the sectarian card to gain political and military support from the GCC neighbours, who helped the Khalifas by sending their forces to intervene in Bahrain. On the other hand, the Khalifa regime snubbed Iran for interfering in Bahrain's internal affairs by supporting the Shia opposition. The Ṣaleh regime in Yemen also played the sectarian card by sidelining the Shias from mainstream Yemeni politics. By using the sectarian card, the regime became a close ally of Saudi Arabia and some other GCC countries for decades. Its close relationship with Saudi Arabia also helped to establish close ties with the USA.

The two main players in the region's sectarian politics, Iran and Saudi Arabia, have used their religious connection with the regimes and the opposition to sway the balance of power in their favour. Iran's close ties with the Shia-dominated regimes of Iraq and Syria provides a boost to its power and influence in the region. Iran's control over Hezbollah gives it a further leverage, which it has been using in the Syrian civil war. Thus the 'Shia Crescent' in the region, consisting of Iran, Iraq, Syria and Hezbollah plays out to Iran's advantage. Further, Iran's alleged connection with and influence over some of the Shia groups such as in Bahrain and Saudi Arabia gives it a strategic advantage in the region. This has been clearly witnessed in the conflicts in the region. Iran has supported the Houthis in Yemen, the Bahraini opposition and the Syrian regime. Similarly, Saudi Arabia plays its sectarian card in the region. The GCC countries as a block add to Saudi Arabia's advantage. In the regional conflicts, Saudi Arabia has supported the Syrian opposition, the Yemeni regime and the Khalifa regime as well.

Resiliency of the Royal Regimes

The authoritarian Arab royal regimes have shown high resiliency while facing popular protests. The outbreak of the Arab Spring, the spread of protests from North Africa to West Asia and the fall of four longstanding leaders, led the people to believe that the traditional Arab world might be crumbling, faced with the wave of popular protests with demands for political, economic and social reforms. But while the rulers of Tunisia, Libya, Egypt and Yemen fell to the street protests, the monarchical regimes in the region have shown a high degree of resiliency. Sean L. Yom and F. Gregory Gause III contend that this 'resilient royalism' flows from the very 'institutional structure' of the Arab state.[5] While countries like Libya, Egypt, Syria and Yemen suffered from poverty and underdevelopment, the monarchies have used their huge oil resources in welfare services of the people.[6] As the protests started spreading in the region, the Gulf monarchies announced large scale welfare measures to appease their citizens. This is a crucial reason for the comparatively lower intensity of protests (except Bahrain) in the Gulf monarchies. The authoritarian nature of the regimes was also another reason for the resiliency of the Gulf regimes. They employed strict military and security measures at the appropriate time to deal with the situation. Also, as the military and the paramilitary forces are commanded by the members of the royal families, there is zero defection in the rank and file of the military. Besides, their strong security partnership with the US acts to their advantage in crisis situations.

Role of the Militaries during Conflict

Militaries have played a crucial role during the Arab Spring. Their support or lack of it has determined the fate of the authoritarian leaders during the protests. In Bahrain, the military was completely under the control of the regime. The sectarian factor played an important role as the Bahraini military is dominated by the Sunnis and the Shia majority is scarcely represented in the military and the security apparatus. The military in Bahrain has exhibited unquestioned loyalty to the royal family. Holger Albrecht and Dorothy Ohl contend that the Bahraini military commanders had an interest in maintaining the status quo, and they believed that the regime's durability was high and individual defections were extremely risky. The commanders' orders were followed by the subordinates, and as a result, the protest was successfully suppressed.[7] The military also believed that they had nothing to gain from regime change.[8] The regime also recruited a large number of Sunnis from foreign countries such as Pakistan, Jordan, etc. in the military, which ensured no military defection in the ranks that would have put the regime in trouble. On the other hand, the Saleh regime in Yemen faced military defections, which weakened Saleh's military capability during the protests. These defections played a major role in weakening the cohesion of the forces loyal to Saleh.[9] At present the pro-Saleh groups have joined with the Houthis and the opposition and are a major force in Yemen.

In Syria, a number of military officers defected and joined the opposition, but the Assad regime still managed to keep enough officers and subordinates. The fact that a large number of top-ranking Syrian military officials are Alawis helped. Most of the subordinates are Sunnis, who are often given orders to control the protesters.[10] Highlighting the difference between the role of the military in Syria and Yemen, Albrecht and Ohl observe:

> "In Syria, horizontal atomized defections of lower-level officers and soldiers helped undermine the army's fighting capacities over time and prop up a fragmented, violent uprising, but it did not lead to the disintegration of the military's organizational infrastructure. Indeed, Al Assad's regime has become too weak to retain control over the country's full territory, but it also remains strong enough not to lose the war. As a result, Syrians suffer through a prolonged civil war without regime change. In Yemen, by contrast, rifts within the political and military elite led to vertical defection patterns, and hence created splits between rival forces. This hastened the government's collapse, and President Saleh's fall in 2011 was also accompanied by the virtual dissolution of the state's coercive apparatus and a 'militia-ization' of the military. The post-Arab Spring Houthi uprising in 2013 therefore did not only trigger civil war, but the very destruction of the regime."[11]

Thus, defections in the militaries have led to losing the grip of the rulers over their control of the security apparatus which was the most powerful means of maintaining the regime security. The rulers of Syria and Yemen suffered losses because of military defection of varying degrees but at the same time the Bahraini rulers were able to ward off the threat of a regime change and to maintain law and order in the aftermath of the protests. In all these countries domestic demographic composition and their representation in the military and security apparatuses have played a crucial role.

Intervention by External Players

Along with the sectarian policies adopted by the regimes and regional players such as Iran and Saudi Arabia, the involvement of the external powers further aggravates the situation. External players intervention has been an important aspect of the West Asia politics and external players have played decisive roles in the region. The history of the region suggests deep involvement of the external players especially by the US in the politics and security of the region. In the region, the regimes are authoritarian and the security challenges are numerous. Occurrence of conflicts and rise of extremist forces are also frequent in West Asia. The regional powers have not been able to manage or resolve the crises which has drawn the the external players into the region. As one scholar notes, without external influence, the regional powers cannot resolve most of the problems created by themselves. The external powers in the region have become an 'integral part of the political landscape' primarily because most of the problems and challenges the regional powers face are either too big for them to handle on their own or were intensified or created by them.[12] In the present crises, along with the US, Russia has also emerged as a major player, especially in the Syrian crisis. Russia's support for the Assad regime has been a game changer not only in the Syrian political scenario but also throughout the region. To worsen things, these external players got the support of either Iran or Saudi Arabia and other regimes and non-state groups in the region.

Tribal Loyalties and Governance System

In Arab societies, people's identities and politics are closely linked to their tribal loyalties. Throughout the Arab world, tribal values, affiliations and culture have shaped the relationship between the state and society. It has been witnessed in numerous instances in history that tribal loyalties have been crucial for survival or fall of ruling elites.

This has been a dominant feature of the tribal Arab societies presently being ruled under authoritarian regimes. As Khaled Fattah notes, in the Arab world, tribal identity is culturally rooted and politically shaped.[13] The Arab Gulf states, Yemen and Iraq are some of the examples of the role of tribal affiliations in the politics of these countries. Fattah observes that there is no fixed pattern of alliance and understanding between the state and the tribal society and leadership. It varies from place to place depending upon the local, social, cultural and economic contexts. But the only fixed feature is that tribes become strong when political administrations are weak and vice versa. He argues that strength of the tribes are closely linked to the weakness of the state.[14] In times of crisis such as the Arab Spring, tribal politics have come to the fore in the region. In crisis situations, the authoritarian rulers hesitated and were reluctant to challenge sectarianism when strong local actors were involved,[15] because the rulers also needed the support of the local tribal leaders for regime security. As Sultan Al Qassemi argues Tribal governance has been a key factor in the domestic politics in the region. Certain positions in the government are allocated to some of the tribal leaders which ensures complete allegiance and loyalty to the ruler.[16]

Growing Trends of Extremism and Terrorism

Widespread violence, extremism and terrorism have been characteristic features of West Asia's sectarian conflicts. The level of violence has increased and has become more pronounced after the outbreak of the Arab Spring. In Syria, a large number of people have joined armed opposition groups against the regime. Also, a number of new extremist and terrorist groups have emerged in the country. ISIS and Jabhat Fateh Al Sham are the deadliest terrorist groups challenging the regime. In its fight against such groups the regime has used heavy force with the military support of allies such as Iran and Russia. In Yemen, the regime has been fighting against the AQAP and the ISIS. Continuing political instability and insecurity help these elements to flourish. The involvement of the Saudi-led military coalition in Yemen has substantially increased the level of violence in the country. There is a growing trend of extremism and violence in Bahrain since the beginning of the protests. Militants have targeted the Bahraini security forces using bombs and other explosive materials. Terrorist organisations such as ISIS and Al Qaeda have been threatening to attack the kingdom as well.

The Rise of ISIS

The rise of ISIS in Iraq and Syria is the most disturbing trend in the whole region. ISIS announced a 'caliphate' in June 2014. ISIS is now fighting the regimes of Iraq and Syria and is growing in numbers as well as operational capability. It has also attacked in Saudi Arabia, Libya, Pakistan, Tunisia, Kuwait and Afghanistan. In Iraq, ISIS continues to have its hold on various cities such as Mosul, Tikrit and Irbil. In Syria, the fight continues between the regime's forces and ISIS to occupy more geographical space. ISIS has attracted extremists from around the world, including a good number of European citizens into its cadres. The rise of ISIS, its capture of territories and attempts to behave like a state by using taxation, etc. is a new trend emerging in the region. Before ISIS, Al-Qaeda was known to be the most dreaded terrorist organisation in the world. But ISIS has surpassed Al-Qaeda in many respects. Al-Qaeda preached for an Islamic *Ummah,* which it never succeeded to establish in any geographical territory. But as ISIS has been able to carve out a geographical territory for itself and is behaving like a state, providing basic services and security it has been able to draw a large number of fighters towards it.

Growing Challenges from Non-state Actors

In West Asia, the states feel more threatened from the non-state actors than from their rival states. For instance, countries such as Iraq, Syria, Yemen, Saudi Arabia face more direct physical threats from the non-state actors in the region more than any of their political rivals. Non-state actors have always been present in the region but their presence and activities have been strengthened since the beginning of the Arab unrest. In some cases the non-state actors are being used by the states for their foreign policy goals. If such trends continue, the challenge from the non-state actors will increase further in the near future. ISIS, Al-Qaeda, Houthis, Hezbollah, Muslim Brotherhood etc. are some of the powerful non-state actors operating in the region today. There is continuous attempt by the non-state actors to expand their influence and activities and are challenged by the military prowess of the states. The states in the region are non-democratic and authoritarian, with strong military and police forces, and therefore, do not hesitate to use force on their citizens, if required. Security of their regimes is top priority for them. So there is a continuous tussle between the non-state actors to expand and the might of the states to counter their advance.

Nexus between Islamists and Regional Powers

The rise of the Islamists and their relationship with the regional powers has impacted the sectarian balance of power in the region. An exciting blend of power politics, ideology and sectarianism is at play in Syria. All the major internal players in Syria are supported by one or other external players. For instance, the Syrian regime has been supported by Iran, Russia and Hezbollah. Similarly, the various rebel groups have also different mentors outside the country including Saudi Arabia, Qatar and other Gulf countries. Muslim Brotherhood is alleged to have strong links with Qatar and Turkey. Similarly, Saudi Arabia has been accused of funding and supporting the Salafi groups in Syria. For Iran, the Lebanese Hezbollah is the most precious asset. The involvement of these powers only leads to strengthening of the different groups and thus leading to further worsening of the conflict.

The Islamists' rise in Syria is also an important reason for the recent conflict within the GCC. Saudi Arabia, UAE and Bahrain recalled their envoys from Qatar alleging Qatar's failure to implement an agreement among GCC countries not to interfere in each other's internal affairs.[17] As mentioned earlier, Saudi Arabia supports the Salafists but Qatar backs the Muslim Brotherhood. There has been an internal tussle between these two countries to increase their power and influence in Syria as both Salafists and the Muslim Brotherhood are actively engaged in opposition to the regime. As the Muslim Brotherhood has played an important role in the formation of the SNC and has been a dominant force in the national coalition it has emerged as a major political force in opposition to the Assad regime. For Saudi Arabia, the Muslim Brotherhood's growing profile in Syria would mean increasing Qatar's influence in Syria and lowering its own role in any future political dispensation in the country. Saudi Arabia has therefore strengthened the Salafi rebels by uniting them to form the Islamic Front, and now it has banned the Muslim Brotherhood as well.

Ever since Morsi's overthrow Saudi Arabia has once again come into the limelight by supporting the Abdel Fattah El Sisi government in Cairo and thereby sidelining the Muslim Brotherhood. The Saudi excitement can be gauged from the fact that immediately after Morsi's overthrow it announced a US$ 5 billion aid package for Egypt in July 2013. Saudi leaders have given statements supporting the post-Morsi developments in Egypt and have not come out openly against the killing of the Muslim Brotherhood supporters on the streets by Egyptian security forces. This is a telling statement. Saudi support for the new regime in Cairo is proportionately related to its disapproval of the Muslim Brotherhood. In the aftermath of the 2012 parliamentary elections, when it became increasingly clear that the Muslim Brotherhood was going to form the next government in Cairo, Saudi Arabia made attempts to accommodate the Muslim Brotherhood in its foreign policy thinking and behaviour. The Muslim Brotherhood emerged as a reality in Egypt, which the Saudis had to accept. On its part, the Muslim Brotherhood also promised to maintain good relations with Riyadh. Nevertheless, the two parties could not build up enough warmth required to establish mutual trust. The Muslim Brotherhood is an ideological challenge to Saudi Arabia's Islamic authority in the world. But the Muslim Brotherhood's popularity on the streets in the post-Mubarak era and the subsequent electoral victory gave it further confidence that it can flourish even without Saudi support, more so as other countries like Qatar were ready to support it politically and financially. Besides, Morsi's attempts to reach out to Tehran did not go down well with Riyadh and made it feel that Morsi could not be a trusted friend in the fluid political environment in the region. As the protests against Morsi gathered momentum, which in turn led to the military's intervention, Saudi Arabia swiftly took the side of the military, viewing it as the right time and opportunity to oust the Muslim Brotherhood from power.

The Muslim Brotherhood in power in Egypt gave Tehran hope for further political gains in the region. The 'Islamic' agenda of the two regimes drew them towards each other. Morsi visited Tehran to participate in the Non Aligned Movement (NAM) meeting in August 2012, the first visit by an Egyptian head of state since 1979. In a similar gesture aimed at improving the bilateral relationship, Iranian President Mahmoud Ahmadinejad visited Egypt in February 2013 to represent his country at the 12th summit of the OIC held in Cairo. But after the overthrow of Morsi, Iran lost a potential friend in the region.

Lack of Political Consensus to Resolve Crises

The aggravation of conflicts between the regimes and the opposition forces in West Asia has diminished the scope of political negotiations to resolve the crises. Yemen and Bahrain held their respective national dialogues to discuss and sort out the issues between the government and the opposition forces. In both cases, the dialogues failed and could not produce any concrete results to build a roadmap for the future. In Yemen, the differences between the government and the opposition forces became extremely acute and the dialogues failed. Dissatisfied with outcomes of the National Dialogue Conference in Yemen, the Houthis started their forward march to capital Sanaa which intensified the conflict in Yemen. With the Houthis capturing the capital and the Saudi-led coalition continuing with its airstrikes, the document of the NDC now remains of least priority. The UN has been making serious efforts to bring all the relevant groups to the negotiating table. But the differences are so huge that it is taking several rounds of negotiations to bring all of them to a consensus. Similarly, in Bahrain also the national dialogue has not been able to fetch any results. The opposition has walked out from the dialogue several times in the past making it even more difficult to reach a consensus. The negotiations continue amidst the regime's violent crackdown on the opposition. The Syrian conflict has drawn the world's attention for a negotiation among the various groups and the regime. The UN has been actively involved in the process of negotiation and trying to bring all the parties to the negotiating table. Kofi Annan's six-point formula has not been adhered to by any of the parties. With all the parties adamant on their respective positions striking a deal is proving to be extremely difficult. Though all the parties to the conflict realise that there is no military solution to conflicts like these, the nature of violence and sectarian polarisation comes as a hindrance in the way of a negotiated political settlement to the crises.

Developments in West Asia affecting World Politics

The developments in Libya, Syria, Iraq and Yemen have to a large extent impacted the global politics. This has directly affected a large number of countries across the continents. Since decades, the US has been playing a dominant role in the region. The involvement of Russia in Syria has added a new dimension to the importance of the region in world politics today. The US-Russia friction over Syria has affected their relationship and the politics at the high table of the UN. The opinion of the international community also remains divided over the involvement of US and Russia in Syria. Further, the impact of the sectarian politics and violence has not remained confined to the boundaries of West Asia. Its impact has been felt across the continents in Africa, Europe, US and South Asia. The migration of millions of refugees to Europe has created both humanitarian and security concerns in Europe. The rise of ISIS has been another deadly challenge which has, beyond the West Asian region, attacked the US, Europe and North African countries. ISIS has been able to attract and radicalise thousands of men and women, which is an alarming trend across continents. Thus, the region is now back to the centre of world politics and will continue to remain a source of insecurity in the foreseeable future.

Into an Uncertain Future

The growing sectarian violence and instability in the region have drawn the regional and extra-regional powers into the conflicts. Their involvement has further widened the boundaries of the conflict. The regional and extra-regional powers have their own set of national interests in the conflicts in the region. The Saudi-Iran rivalry and competition would remain one of the major determinants of regional stability in West Asia. The Arab Spring has further widened the gulf between these two countries and the recent escalations point towards a long-term confrontation between them. The political, ideological and strategic contentions have also shaped the internal conflicts in the countries of the region. Both countries have used sectarianism as a foreign policy tool to pursue their interests in the region and in the absence of any dialogue mechanism between them the sectarian card will be played more often in the future. Religious extremism and terrorism of various shades have grown exponentially and moderate voices have been pushed aside. The extremist voices are likely to grow if the chaotic political environment continues in the near future.

The politics of sectarian alliances are also likely to continue in the foreseeable future. Determined efforts by Iran and Saudi Arabia to bring the regimes and opposition groups to their side have resulted in the sectarian divide becoming more pronounced. The involvement of extra-regional players with the regional actors as well as the local opposition forces and militias leads to an even more complex situation. Such nexus has been witnessed in Syria, Bahrain, Yemen and other places in the region. Such alliances based on sectarian affiliations and strategic calculations will only give further impetus to the regional instability.

The Arab Spring, which has led to regime changes, unremitting violence and political instability, has not been able to meet the aspirations and demands of the people. The demands for political reforms, economic equality, employment opportunities, ending social discrimination etc. remain to be addressed. The rulers have focussed their attention and energy on merely securing their regimes and maintaining law and order. The protesting youths, who have wanted to have a say in the affairs of the state, better employment opportunities and an egalitarian society, remain disillusioned with the responses of the regimes. This is a distressing sign for the region as a whole as the youths may come to the streets in future again with their demands.

In the coming years, the conflicts and political instability in West Asia will be determined by a complex set of forces and actors at play at the local, regional and global levels. The internal demographic dynamics has been used by the regimes and oppositions alike to garner the support of various groups, tribes and sects. The Arab unrest has exposed the sectarian sensitivities of the rulers as well as the citizens. Sectarian sentiments have taken a political shape, the repercussions of which have been extremely dangerous. Sectarian forces have played a determining role in the present conflict and seem to remain powerful in the foreseeable future as well.

END NOTES

1. Daniel Byman, "Sectarianism Afflicts the New Middle East", *Survival: Global Politics and Strategy*, 56 (1), 2014, p. 84.
2. Mahdi Mohammad Nia and Abdolmajid Seifi "The Ideational Nature of Iranian-Saudi Interactions", *Iranian Review of Foreign Affairs*, 5 (4), Winter 2015, pp. 91-117.
3. Mohamed Bin Huwaidin, "The security dilemma in Saudi-Iranian relations", *Review of History and Political Science*, 3 (2), December 2015, pp. 69-79.
4. Ibid., p. 77.
5. Sean L. Yom and F. Gregory Gause III, "Resilient royals: How Arab monarchies hang on", *Journal of Democracy*, 23 (4), October 2012, p. 77.
6. Ibid., p. 83.
7. Holger Albrecht and Dorothy Ohl, "Exit, resistance, loyalty: Military behavior during unrest in authoritarian regimes", *Perspectives on Politics*, 14 (1), March 2016, p. 44.
8. Sharon Erickson Nepstad, "Mutiny and nonviolence in the Arab Spring: Exploring military defections and loyalty in Egypt, Bahrain, and Syria", *Journal of Peace Research*, 50 (3), 2013, p. 344.
9. Michael Knights, "The military role in Yemen's protests: Civil-military relations in the tribal republic", *Journal of Strategic Studies*, 36 (2), 2013, pp. 261-288.
10. Nepstad, n. 8, p. 344.
11. Albrecht and Ohl, n. 7, p. 48.
12. P.R. Kumaraswamy, "A love-hate relationship: External interventions and Middle East", in Prasanta Kumar Pradhan (ed.), *Geopolitical Shifts in West Asia: Trends and Implications*, Pentagon Press and IDSA, New Delhi, 2016, pp. 124-147.
13. Khaled Fattah, "Tribes and tribalism in the Arab Spring", *Yemen Times*, April 26, 2012, at http://www.yementimes.com/en/1567/variety/760/Tribes-and-tribalism-in-the-Arab-Spring.htm
14. Ibid.
15. Daniel Byman, n. 1, p. 85.
16. Sultan Al Qassemi, "Tribalism in the Arabian Peninsula: It Is a Family Affair", *Jadaliyya*, February 1, 2012, at http://www.jadaliyya.com/pages/index/4198/tribalism-in-the-arabian-peninsula_it-is-a-family-
17. "KSA, Bahrain, UAE recall ambassadors from Qatar", *Arab News*, March 5, 2014, at http://www.arabnews.com/news/535101.

Index